MacBook Air
Beginners and Seniors

2019 Updated Manual to Operate Your Computer on macOS Catalina

Tech Analyst

Copyright @2019

TABLE OF CONTENT

How to Use this Book 10

Introduction 11

iTunes Split into TV, Music, and Podcasts 12

Sidecar as a Second Screen 13

Auto Dark Mode 14

Improved Photos App 14

The Notes App 14

Reminders App 15

Screen Time 15

Safari 16

Find My 16

New Accessibility Features 16

Improvement of Security and Privacy 17

Chapter 1: Getting Started 18

Download and Install macOS Catalina 18

Erase a Partition on Your Mac 19

Create a Partition to Install macOS Catalina 20

Removing a Partition on Your Mac 21

Switching Between Partitions 22

Downgrade to the Previous Operating System 22

Chapter 2: Screen Time in macOS Catalina 26

Enabling Screen Time 26

Disable Screen Time 27

Add Password to Screen Time 28

Share Screen Time Across All Devices 29

View Notifications Sent in Screen Time 30

View App Usage in Screen Time 31

Viewing Device Pickups in Screen Time 31

Set Limits Using Screen Time 32

Remove App Limits 33

Schedule Downtime Using Screen Time 33

Always Allowed Contents in Screen Time 34

Content and Privacy Using Screen Time 35

Automatically Run Dark Mode 36

Find a Lost Device with the 'Find My' App 37

Track Friends with Find My App 38

Track Your Device with Find My App 39

Chapter 3: Syncing your iPad/ iPhone with Your Mac 40

Where to Sync your iPad and iPhone on macOS Catalina
.... 40

Sync Movies Between your iPad or iPhone on macOS Catalina 40

Sync Music to Your iPad or iPhone on Mac 41

Sync TV Shows to your iPad or iPhone on Mac 42

Sync Audiobooks to your iPad or iPhone on Mac 43

Sync Podcasts to your iPad or iPhone on Mac 44

Sync Books to your iPad or iPhone on Mac 45

Sync Files to your iPad or iPhone on Mac 46

Sync Photos to your iPad or iPhone on Mac 47

Back-up your iPad or iPhone on macOS Catalina 47

Restore your iPad or iPhone on Mac 48

Chapter 4: Music App 49

Using Apple Music in the Music App 49

Play Music in the Music App 51

Access Your Music Library in the Music App 52

Get Album and Song Info in the Music App 54

Import Music into the Music App 55

General Settings in the Music App 56

Playback Settings in the Music App 57

Setting up Parental Controls in the Music App 59

Music File Settings 61

Reset Warnings in the Music App 63

Chapter 5: Podcasts App on Mac 65

Play a Podcast in the Podcast App 65

Search for Podcast from your Podcast Library 65

Search for a Podcast from the App 66

Subscribe to a Podcast 67

Unsubscribe to a Podcast 68

Play a Podcast Next in Queue from the App 69

Delete a Podcast from Your Podcast Library 70

Share a Podcast in the App 71

4

View Top Charts in the Podcasts App 72

Change the Play Order of Episodes 73

Chapter 6: Apple TV App for Mac 75

Play a Video from Your Library in the TV App 75

Watch a Movie or Show in the TV App 77

Add Movies and Shows to Up Next 78

Buy TV Shows and Movies in the TV app 79

Subscribe to a Channel in the TV App 80

Cancel a Channel Subscription on Your Mac 81

Video Playback Settings in the TV App 81

Downloads in the TV Apps 82

Manage Media Files in the TV App 83

Reset Warnings, Clear Cache and Play History 85

Setting up Parental Controls in the TV App 85

Chapter 7: Notes App on Mac 87

Starting a New Note 87

Make a Checklist 87

Reorder Checklist Notes 88

Make a Dashed, Bulleted or Numbered Headings and List
.... 88

Create Password for Locked Notes 89

View Note Attachments 90

Lock a Note 90

Sign in to iCloud 91

5

Invite Others to Collaborate on a Note 92

Send Note to Another App or Person 93

View Notes in a Gallery 93

Sync Notes to iCloud in macOS Catalina 94

Chapter 8: Reminders App on Mac 95

Create a Reminder 95

Add Reminders Account Provider 95

Setting up Location Notification for a Reminder 97

Schedule Due Date for a Reminder 97

Create a New List 98

Rename a List 98

Delete a List 98

Share a List with Another iCloud User 99

Move a Reminder to another List 100

Using Text Snippets in Reminder 100

Group Reminder Lists 101

Add a Message Notification for Reminders 101

Add Attachments to Reminder 102

Add Secondary Reminder to an Existing one 104

Chapter 9: Voice Controls on Mac 105

Turn on Voice Control 105

Change the Voice Control Language on Mac 105

Sleep/ Wake Voice Control on Mac 106

Select New Language in Voice Control 106

Choose a Different Microphone for Voice Control 107
Disable/ Enable Commands in Voice Control 107
Create Custom Commands in Voice Control 108
Delete Custom Commands in Voice Control 109
Receive an Alert for Recognized Commands in Voice Control 110
Chapter 10: Using Sidecar on Mac 111
Requirements to Use Sidecar 111
Setting up Sidecar on Mac 112
Setting up Sidecar on your iPad 112
Customize Sidecar on your Computer 113
Customizing Apple Pencil Options 114
The iPad as a Graphics Tablet 114
Chapter 11: Mail App 115
Setting up an Email account 115
Setting Frequency for Searching for New Messages 116
Mail Notification Sounds 117
Add a Signature to your Emails 117
Sending a new Email 118
Replying an Email 119
Download and View Email Attachments 120
Searching for Specific Email Messages 120
Filter Email by Unread 121
Mark an Email as Unread 122

Deleting an Email 122

Apple Mail Flag Feature 123

Unsubscribe from a Mailing List in Mail 123

Block a Sender in Mail 124

Sign Documents on Your Computer with your iPad or iPhone in Quick Look 125

Sign Documents on Your Computer with your iPad or iPhone in Preview 126

Chapter 12: Safari on Mac 128

Steps to Use Picture-in-Picture Feature in Safari 128

Visit a Website 129

Bookmark a Website 129

Searching on the Address Bar 130

Remove Bookmarks 131

View All Bookmarks 131

Add a Web Page to your Reading List 132

Enable Private Browsing 132

View Your Reading List 133

Remove items from your Reading Lists 133

Add Extensions to Safari 134

Pin Tabs on Safari 135

Setting Browser Homepage 136

Reader View 137

Share Websites from Safari 137

Change Background Color in Reader View 138

Modify Font Size in Reader View 138

Modify Font in Reader View 139

Customize Favorites in Safari 139

Organize Your Safari Favorites 140

Organize Frequently Visited in Safari 140

Access Siri Suggestions 141

Chapter 13: Conclusion 142

How to Use this Book

Welcome! Thank you for purchasing this book and trusting us to lead you right in operating macOS Catalina on your MacBook Pro. This book has covered every detail and tip you need to know about macOS Catalina to get the best from your computer.

To better understand how the book is structured, I will advise you read from page to page, after which you can then navigate to particular sections as well as refer to topics individually. This book has been written in the simplest form to ensure that every user understands and gets the best out of this book. The table of content is also well outlined to make it easy for you to reference topics as needed at the speed of light.

Thank you.

Introduction

In July 2019, Apple refreshed the MacBook Air, which was initially launched in October 2018. While there are no significant differences between the 2018 model and the 2019 model, the updated version came at a reduced price, included some minor SSD changes, an updated display with True Tone as well as a new butterfly keyboard designed with the same materials as the 2019 model of the MacBook Pro.

On October 7, 2019, the Apple company introduced an upgrade from the macOS Mojave to the macOS Catalina, which is available for download and installation on the MacBook Air computers. Regardless of the year of your MacBook Air computer, you can enjoy the features of this new operating system.

With the introduction of the macOS Catalina, you now have more features to explore on your Macbook Air like the **Picture in Picture** feature, New Dark Mode, Apple Arcade, option to unsubscribe directly in the Mail app and lots more. Even for existing users, these new features may seem a little overwhelming when using them for the first time.

In this user guide, you would find detailed steps on how to explore every available addition to the macOS Catalina along with pictures to make it easy for you to understand and follow. Whether you are just buying a new MacBook Air or downloading the latest software to your existing device, this book has all you need to achieve more productivity on your Mac computer.

iTunes Split into TV, Music, and Podcasts

For some time now, we heard the rumor that the iTunes will be overhauled, and this happened with macOS Catalina after the Apple announcement in June 2019. iTunes app has been divided into three individual apps: TV, Music, and Podcasts. Apple's aim for doing this is to make it easier for developers to build apps that can work on both iOS and macOS. Rather than have two separate sets of codes, developers now need to tick only one checkbox for their macOS app to become an iOS one and vice versa. To sync your iPhone in the absence of the iTunes, connect your smartphone to your Mac and you will see all the syncing options displayed in the Finder Sidebar.

Sidecar as a Second Screen

While iOS is not merging with Mac, the new software has made it possible for both of them to collaborate. This feature is what Apple called **Sidecar**. The sidecar has two sides. On the first side, your iPad can serve as a second screen for your Mac using the Sidecar. As soon as you pair both devices, you can move a window to your iPad from your Mac, which could be quite useful for reference purposes when working on a document. The Sidecar creates a sidebar on the iPad device that you can use to access the Control, Command and Shift keys. You can also use this to activate the Touch Bar on your iPad when needed.

The second part of the Sidecar feature is that you can use your iPad as a markup and drawing device for your Mac. This simply means that you can mirror a document on your iPad from the Mac, then use the Apple Pencil to make drawings on this document, and it will show on the Mac. Before now, the only way you could achieve this was to get something like the Wacom tablet but the new software has made this easier.

Auto Dark Mode

You can now automatically adjust the Dark and Light mode to suit the time of the day. The Dark Mode is a setting that applies to the whole system so it will reflect on the desktop as well as all your settings windows, Apple apps, and any third-party app that has the feature enabled. This means you do not have to stress by clicking and manually changing the feature.

Improved Photos App

Some new features were added to the Photos app like the new gallery view that arranges your pictures into tiles of different sizes while hiding the clutter in your library and presenting your best shots first. You can now browse your photos by the month, day, and year it was captured as the app makes use of machine learning to bring out your best shots within each period.

The Notes App

The Notes app also has a new gallery view that displays the thumbnails for your notes, to give you a quick view of each of your notes, and their contents. If you need to work with other persons on a shared Notes collection, you can create a shared folder for this. Also, it is now easier and faster to use the search function of the app.

Another feature is the new checklist feature that allows you to set some notes as completed. Once the notes are marked as completed, they move to the bottom of the list so that you can concentrate on the incomplete ones.

Reminders App

The reminders app was overhauled in the new software. It comes refreshed with new features that users will find helpful. The app now understands text snippets like the time and date of a reminder, and it can automatically create smart lists. Siri can also suggest reminders based on the content of the Messages app.

Screen Time

Screen Time has been on iOS but just got to Mac with macOS Catalina. With this feature, you can limit the duration of time you spend on the internet, apps and even the Mac itself. This feature aims to help you place priority and focus on what needs to be done. When you launch the Screen Time, it will show you in detail the amount of time you spend on your Mac for different apps. With that, you can know what takes your time on your device and what you need to cut down. From the App limit section, you can specify the duration of time to spend on an app.

Safari

The Safari browser has a new start page that shows both your favorites as well as frequently visited sites. This will make it faster for you to access your most liked sites. Siri's suggestions will also come up on the home screen to include links and bookmarks from your reading list, links that came in via messages, iCloud tabs, and lots more.

Find My

Apple recently combined the **Find My Friends and Find My iPhone** into a single app they called the **Find My** in iOS 13, iPadOS and MacOS Catalina. You can use this new feature to find both your friends and your devices. For all your friends that may have shared their location with you, you can navigate to the People section to see their location at the time. With this new feature, you can find your device even if it is offline, due to the encrypted, anonymous Bluetooth signal that the device sends out periodically.

New Accessibility Features

macOS Catalina brings its addition to the accessibility features. For one, the Voice Control feature allows you to use your voice to operate your Mac. You can tell your

Mac what you will like to do at a given time. the ability to zoom text on a second r maintaining the normal zoom level on the You can also hover on a text and click control to enlarge the text for easy reading.

Improvement of Security and Privacy

Apple is always concerned about safeguarding the privacy of its users, and the company maintained this in her newest software. macOS Catalina has its read-only volume on the Mac drive that helps to keep the system files protected from being overwritten. Another thing is that apps will need your full permission before they can access files in Desktop and Documents folders, external and iCloud Drives.

Apple has further integrated the Apple watch with the Mac. For those that have an Apple watch, you can authorize stuff like payments on your Mac by clicking twice on your Watch's side button. You can use this for opening locked notes, viewing passwords in Safari and approving app installations.

Chapter 1: Getting Started

Download and Install macOS Catalina

Ensure to back up your Mac before you begin the upgrade.

- Go to the App store on your Mac, search for macOS Catalina.
- Click on the button to begin the installation.
- When you see a pop-up window on your screen, click on **Continue** to start the download.
- The download will go straight to your application folder.
- As soon as the download is done, the installer will launch
- Then follow the instructions on your screen to install the new software to your Mac.
- You may need to input the administrator name and password, when asked during installation.

You can also download and install the new software from your system settings with the steps below:

- On the left upper side of your screen, click on the Apple icon.

- Select **System Preferences.**

- Click on **Software Updates**
- Then tap **Update Now**

Erase a Partition on Your Mac

Before you take any step, ensure to back up your system. Then restart your computer in the primary partition to enable you to erase the extra ones.

- Go to your dock and launch **Finder.**
- Click on **Applications.**
- Move down and click on the **Utilities** folder.
- Click twice to launch the **Disk Utility.**
- Choose the partition you want to cleanout.
- Then click on **Erase.**
- Click on **Erase** again to confirm your decision.
- Then click on **Done.**

Create a Partition to Install macOS Catalina

You can decide to run both macOS Catalina and Mojave on your computer at the same time as Apple has made it easy with the built-in disk utility program. The steps below will show you how to partition your computer. To partition your computer means splitting the hard drive into separate systems that are usable. It allows you to run two different operating systems on a single device, like having both macOS Mojave and Catalina in one single computer or macOS and Windows. Please note that when you partition your hard drive, you are also splitting the available hard drive space. So, I will not advise you to do this if you do not have sufficient hard drive space. Ensure that you have backed up your computer before you start and also confirm that you have enough free space for the second operating system, at least 30GB free for a start.

- Go to your dock and launch **Finder.**
- Click on **Applications.**
- Move down and click on the **Utility** folder.
- Click twice to launch the **Disk Utility.**
- From the Disk Utility window, click on your hard drive, usually named "Macintosh HD" or "Fusion."

- Then click on the **Partition section.**
- You will receive a prompt to either add a Partition or an APFS volume
- Select **Partition.**
- Then click on the (+) sign to Add Partition.
- Drag the resize control to the left or right to modify the size of the partition you want to use; the blue color represents used space.
- Type your preferred name for the new partition.
- Confirm the file system format for the new partition. For macOS Catalina, select APFS.
- Then click on **Apply**
- Allow some minutes for disk utility to effect the changes.

Removing a Partition on Your Mac

After you must have erased the partition, you can now remove it from your hard drive.

- Click on the primary partition, which is the first drive you will see on the list. Its often called "Macintosh HD" or "Fusion."
- Click on **Partition.**
- Choose the Partition to remove

- Tap the (-) button
- Then click on **Apply**
- This may take some minutes as Disk Utility checks the disks to make changes.

Switching Between Partitions

The steps below will show you how to move between two partitions:

- Click on the Apple icon at the left top side of your screen.
- Then click on **System Preferences** from the available options on the list.
- Click on **Startup Disk**
- Tap the **Lock** icon at the left lower corner of your screen to unlock and make your changes.
- Input your admin password then click **OK**
- Choose your Partition Drive
- Then click on **Restart.**

Downgrade to the Previous Operating System

Step 1: Backup Your Mac

It is vital to back up your computer before you delete macOS Catalina from your hard drive. Deleting Catalina will erase any programs, files or documents that you did not back up. You can back up to an external drive or cloud-based applications like iCloud, OneDrive/ DropBox.

Step 2: Make a Bootable Drive for the macOS Mojave

First, download the macOS Mojave from your computer's app store before deleting macOS Catalina. Store the Mojave in an external hard drive.

Step 3: Delete macOS Catalina

Follow the steps below for this

- Connect your system to an active Wi-Fi or ethernet
- Then tap the Apple icon at the left top side of your screen.
- Click on **Restart** from the available options.
- Press down the **Command+R** keys, continue to hold until your system reboots. Your computer will now enter Recovery Mode.
- From OS X Utilities selector, click on **Disk Utility.**
- Select **Continue**
- Choose your **Startup Disk**
- Go to the window top and click on **Erase.**
- Input a name for the file you want to delete (macOS Catalina)

- Choose APFS from the list or **Mac OS Extended**
- Then click on **GUID Partition Map** if **Scheme** is available.
- Click on **Erase**
- Once done, click on **Quit Disk Utility** from the available menu in the left top side of your screen to return to the OS X Utilities selector.

Step 4: Reinstall macOS Mojave

- Connect your system to an active Wi-Fi or Ethernet
- Plug in the bootable hard drive where macOS Mojave is stored, into your computer.
- Then click on the Apple icon at the left top side of your screen.
- Choose **Restart** from the list.
- Press down on **Options** as the system restarts. This will take you to Options to choose a startup disk.
- From the list of the startup disks, choose your bootable drive that has macOS Mojave saved. macOS Mojave will begin to install on your computer.

- Click on **Continue** in the installation window.
- Agree to the terms and the software will then reboots your system.

Step 5: Restore your backup

- Connect your system to an active Wi-Fi or Ethernet
- Then click on the Apple icon at the left top side of your screen.
- Choose **Restart** from the list.
- As soon as you hear the chime sound upon startup, press down the **Command+R** keys. Continue to hold until the system reboots.
- Click on **Restore from Time Machine Backup**
- Then click on **Continue.**
- Click on **Continue** again as soon as you have read the info about restoring the backup.
- Choose the backup source where the backup is stored.
- Click on **Continue.**
- Click on the latest backup on the drive
- Then click on **Continue.**

- Your computer will start to restore the backup and then reboot.

Chapter 2: Screen Time in macOS Catalina

While screen time has been available in iOS since 2018, it is only just getting to Mac. With Screen time, you are able to set up restrictions on how you use your device from setting up an app curfew on the devices belonging to your kids to blocking distracting notifications. The Screen Time is mostly used to block certain websites and apps that you use more often than is needed. This will give you the time to concentrate on other important things that needs to be done without the temptation of going to the blocked app or website, say for instance, Instagram. The steps below will show you how to enable this option.

Enabling Screen Time

- Go to **System Preferences**
    - Then click on **Screen Time.**

- Navigate to the bottom left and click on **Options.**
- Then click on **Turn On,** located at the right top side of your screen, to begin using screen time.

Disable Screen Time

- Go to **System Preferences**
- Then click on **Screen Time.**
- Navigate to the bottom left and click on **Options**

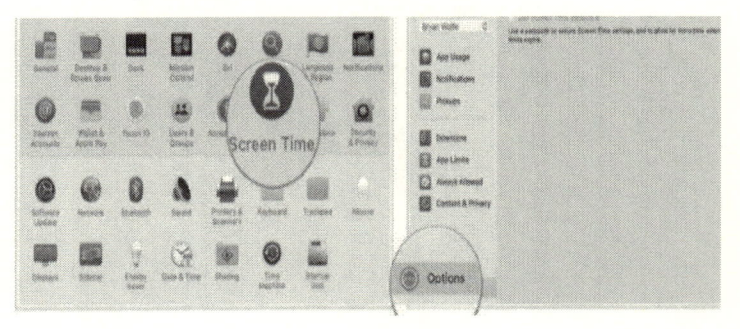

- Then click on **Turn Off,** located at the right top side of your screen, to stop using screen time.

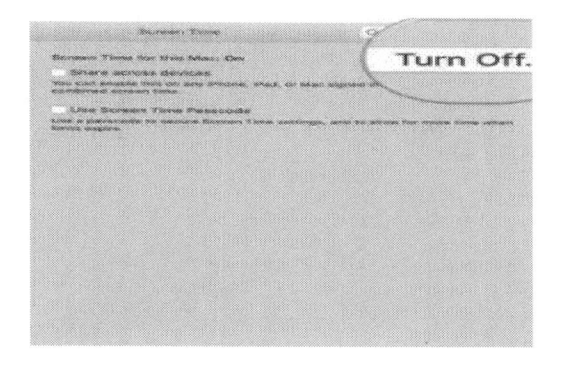

Add Password to Screen Time

Adding a password to this feature will help to keep your settings safe and the password can also be used to extend screen time for other users when needed.

- Go to **System Preferences**
- Then click on **Screen Time.**
- Navigate to the bottom left and click on **Options**
- Check the box for **Use Screen Time Password,** and set your preferred password.

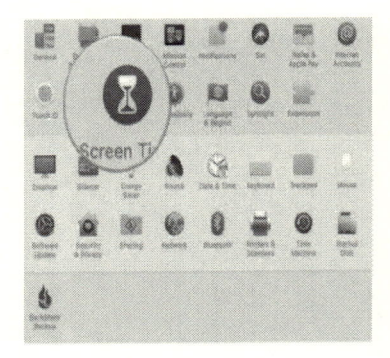

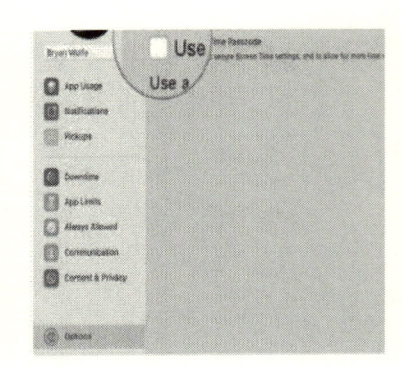

Share Screen Time Across All Devices

To give you complete details on the total time you spend online, you can make use of the Screen Time feature on all your Apple devices. When you do this, you can see your total Screen Time across all your devices on this app. Follow the steps below to enable this option

- Go to **System Preferences**
- Then click on **Screen Time.**
- Navigate to the bottom left and click on **Options.**
- Then click on **Share Across Devices**.

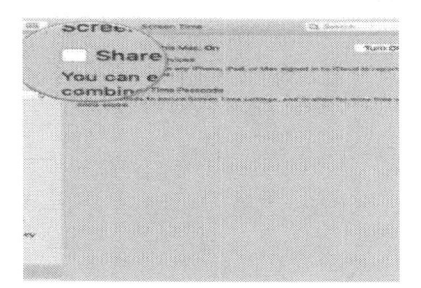

View Notifications Sent in Screen Time

If you want to know where your notifications are coming from, you can see that info from the Screen Time view.

- Go to **System Preferences**
- Then click on **Screen Time.**
- From the left side of the screen, click on **Notifications.**
- You will then see which apps sent notifications and the total number of received notifications by the day or week.

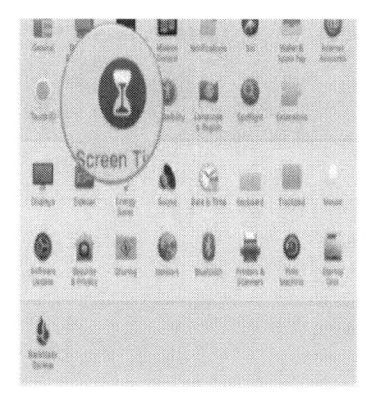

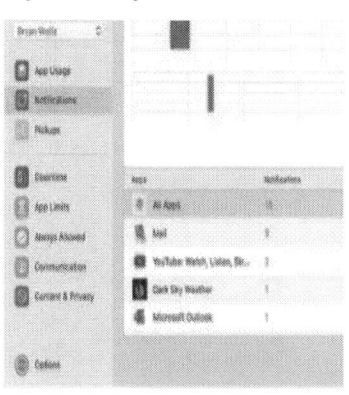

View App Usage in Screen Time

- Go to **System Preferences**
- Then click on **Screen Time.**
- Navigate to the left and click on **App Usage**
- On the next screen, you will see your app usage displayed by days, categories and apps. You will also find apps with limit on this screen.

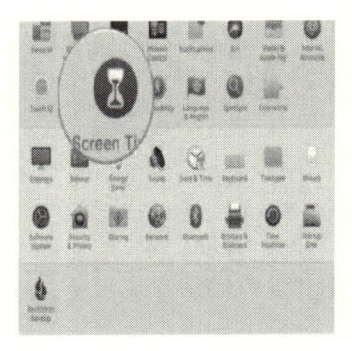

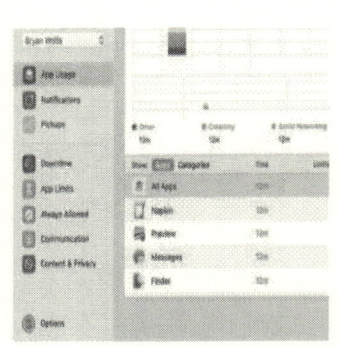

Viewing Device Pickups in Screen Time

If you have enabled the option to share the Screen Time across all your Apple devices, you can go to the Mac app to see the number of times you have picked up your mobile devices.

- Go to **System Preferences**
- Then click on **Screen Time.**

- At the left side of your screen, click on **Pickups**

Set Limits Using Screen Time

This setting allows you to choose the time limit for each app categories.

- Go to **System Preferences**
- Then click on **Screen Time.**
- At the left side of your screen, click on **App Limits.**
- Then click on **Turn On** to enable App Limits.
- Click on the **(+)** to add an app category.
- Then tick the box beside the app categories you want to place a limit.
- After the app category has been highlighted, use the radio buttons to set your limits. You can choose either **Custom** or **Every Day.**
- Repeat the last two steps above for each category you want to place a limit.
- Then click on **Done** to confirm your selection.

33

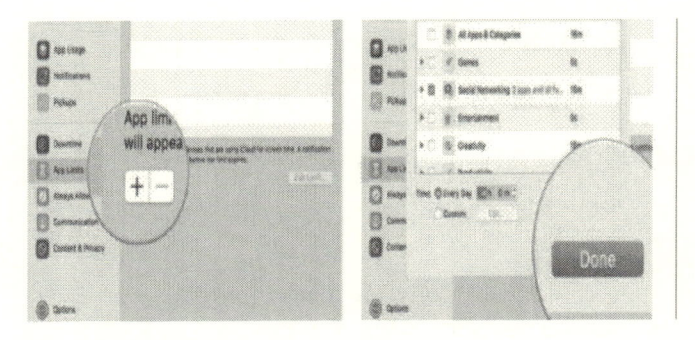

Remove App Limits

- Go to **System Preferences**
- Then click on **Screen Time.**
- At the left side of your screen, click on **App Limits**
- For each category you want to lift the limit, untick the box beside it at the right.
- Click on **Turn Off** to disable app tracking.

Schedule Downtime Using Screen Time

Whenever Downtime is enabled, the only things that can work on your Mac are apps that you have given permission to work as well as phone calls. Follow the steps below to set up your downtime schedule

- Go to **System Preferences**
- Then click on **Screen Time.**

- From the left side of the screen, click on **Downtime.**
- Then click on **Turn On** to enable downtime
- Use the radio button to select either **Custom** or **Every Day** depending on your preferred schedule.
- If you select **Every Day,** it means that Downtime should happen at same time every day while the **Custom** option means that you can modify the time for different days of the week and even untick a box beside a particular day to disable **Downtime** for that day.

Always Allowed Contents in Screen Time

This setting allows you to make some certain processes available every time regardless of any existing restrictions. These processes may include communication with some apps or people. The steps below will show you how to set the **Always Allowed** feature

- Go to **System Preferences**
- Then click on **Screen Time.**

- At the left side of your screen, click on **Always Allowed.**

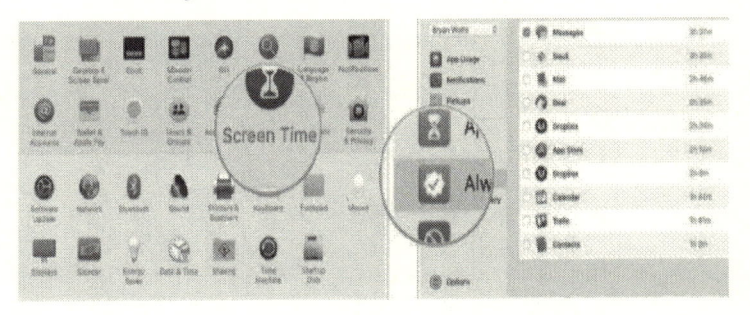

- Tick the box beside each of the desired items to **Always Allow**

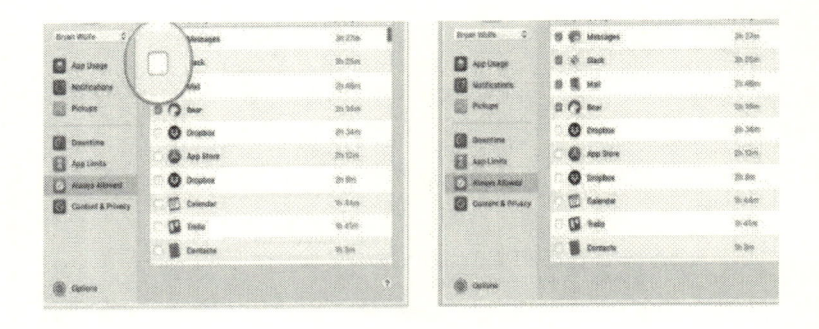

Content and Privacy Using Screen Time

You can go through the Screen Time app to set your content and privacy with the steps below:

- Go to **System Preferences**
- Then click on **Screen Time.**

- On the left side of your screen, click on **Contents and Privacy.**
- To enable the Content and privacy option, click on **Turn On.**
- You will find four options there: Apps, Stores, Content and Other. Tick each of the displayed boxes under each of the four options

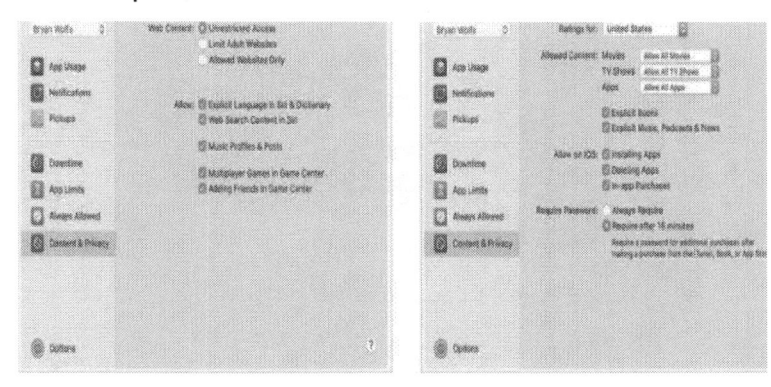

Automatically Run Dark Mode

A new feature called **Dark Mode** has been introduced with macOS Catalina to bring a beautiful new color scheme to your Mac laptop. This feature has only two options: it is either enabled or disabled. What this means is that you can turn on or off the Dark Mode automatically depending on the time of the day, such that, as soon as the sun goes down, the operating system in your Mac will turn to a classy dark theme to make it easy for your eyes to adjust. As soon as the sun is up, the light theme returns. Follow the simple steps below to enable this option:

- Go to **System Preferences**

- Click on **General.**
- At the top of your screen, you will see the section for **Appearance.**
- Click on **Auto** to automatically run Dark Mode.
- If you prefer your Mac to be permanently on the Dark or Light theme, you can select your preference from this screen rather than choosing **Auto.**

Find a Lost Device with the 'Find My' App

The "Find My" app was announced during the Worldwide Developer's Conference that held in July

2019. This feature makes use of anonymized snippets of data transmitted from one Mac device to another until you can locate your missing device. The steps below will guide you on how to do this:

- To launch the 'Find My' app, press **Cmd + Space** and then type **'Find My'** in the Spotlight.
- At the left top corner of your screen, click on **Devices.**
- Then select the missing device.
- The missing device will show on the map.
- Click on the **'i'** button on the map to display a list of options.
- Click on **Directions** to get to your missing device.

Track Friends with Find My App

When you go to the People section on the Find My app, you will see all the people that you have access to track.

- Go to the People's tab in the Find My app.
- On the left side of the screen, you have names of people you can track. Click on your preference.
- You have the option to view on three maps: satellite, hybrid, and default.

- Use the plus (+) and minus (-) icon to modify the map size.
- Click on the location icon to display your current location.
- Tap the button for **Share My Location** to share your location with a new contact.
- Go to the 'To' field and input the receiver name.
- For receivers not saved in your contacts, use the pop-up menu to add them.
- After adding the new receiver, click on **Send**.

Track Your Device with Find My App

- Go to the **Devices** tab in the Find My app.
- On the left side of the screen, click on the device you want to track.
- You have the option to view on three maps: satellite, hybrid, and default.
- Use the plus (+) and minus (-) icon to modify the map size.
- Click on the location icon to display your current location.

Chapter 3: Syncing your iPad/ iPhone with Your Mac

Even with the absence of iTunes, you can still sync your mobile devices with your Mac computer.

Where to Sync your iPad and iPhone on macOS Catalina

Rather than syncing your mobile device with iTunes, you will now use Finder on your Mac.

- From your Dock, click on the Finder app.
- Click on the name of your device on the left side of your screen.
- As soon as you click on this, you will see the interface that you are familiar with from the macOS Mojave.
- You can now manage backups, restore your device, or sync content between the mobile device and your computer. You can also carry out file transfers from one device to the other on this screen.

Sync Movies Between your iPad or iPhone on macOS Catalina

- From your Dock, click on the Finder app.

- Click on the name of your device on the left side of your screen.
- Click on the **Movies** tab on the right side of your screen.
- To enable movie syncing, tick the box beside **Sync Movies onto your device**
- Under sync options, tick the box for **Automatically include**.
- From the pull-down menu, choose **All** to select every content or pick specific options from the list.
- Click on **Apply**
- Then click on **Sync** at the right bottom of the screen to sync your movies between your mobile device and the Mac.

Sync Music to Your iPad or iPhone on Mac

Note: You cannot sync music on your Mac if using iCloud Music library sync on your iPad or iPhone.

- From your Dock, click on the Finder app.
- Click on the name of your device on the left side of your screen.

- Click on the Music tab on the right side of your screen.
- To enable music syncing, tick the box beside **Sync Music onto your device**
- Under sync options, you can choose either "**Selected playlists, artists, albums, and genres**" or "**Entire music library.**"
- Go to **Options,** and tick the box beside "**Automatically fill free space with songs**" and "**Include Videos**" only if you want.
- Then click on **playlists, albums, artists, and genre**, if applicable
- Click on **Apply**
- Then click on **Sync** at the right bottom of the screen to sync your music files between your mobile device and the Mac

Sync TV Shows to your iPad or iPhone on Mac

- From your Dock, click on the Finder app.
- Click on the name of your device on the left side of your screen.
- Click on the **TV shows** tab on the right side of your screen.

- To enable **TV shows** syncing, tick the box beside **Sync TV shows onto your device**
- Under sync options, tick the box for **Automatically include**.
- From the pull-down menu, choose **All Unwatched** to select every content or pick specific options from the list.
- From the next pull-down menu, choose either **selected shows** or **all shows**.
- If you clicked on **Selected Shows,** then tick the boxes beside the shows you wish to sync.
- Click on **Apply**
- Then click on **Sync** at the right bottom of the screen to sync your TV shows between your mobile device and the Mac.

Sync Audiobooks to your iPad or iPhone on Mac

- From your Dock, click on the Finder app.
- Click on the name of your device on the left side of your screen.
- Click on the **Audiobooks** tab on the right side of your screen.

- To enable **Audiobook** syncing, tick the box beside **Sync Audiobooks onto your device**.
- Under sync option, choose either **selected Audiobooks** or **all Audiobooks**.
- If you clicked on **Selected Audiobooks,** then tick the boxes beside the audiobooks you wish to sync.
- Click on **Apply**
- Then click on **Sync** at the right bottom of the screen to sync your audiobooks between your mobile device and the Mac

Sync Podcasts to your iPad or iPhone on Mac
- From your Dock, click on the Finder app.
- Click on the name of your device on the left side of your screen.
- Click on the **Podcasts** tab at the right side of your screen.
- To enable **Podcasts** syncing, tick the box beside **Sync Podcasts onto your device**.
- Then tick the box beside **Automatically copy**.

- From the pull-down menu, choose "**All unplayed**" to select every content or pick specific options from the list.
- From the next pull-down menu, choose either **selected shows** or **all podcasts**.
- If you clicked on **Selected podcasts,** then tick the boxes beside the podcasts you wish to sync.
- Click on **Apply**
- Then click on **Sync** at the right bottom of the screen to sync your podcasts between your mobile device and the Mac.

Sync Books to your iPad or iPhone on Mac

- From your Dock, click on the Finder app.
- Click on the name of your device on the left side of your screen.
- Click on the **Books** tab on the right side of your screen.
- To enable **Books** syncing, tick the box beside **Sync Books onto your device**.
- Under sync option, choose either **selected books** or **all books**.

- If you clicked on **Selected books,** then tick the boxes beside the books you wish to sync.
- Click on **Apply**
- Then click on **Sync** at the right bottom of the screen to sync your books between your mobile device and the Mac.

Sync Files to your iPad or iPhone on Mac

- From your Dock, click on the Finder app.
- Click on the name of your device on the left side of your screen.
- Click on the **Files** tab on the right side of your screen.
- To enable **Files** syncing, tick the box beside **Sync Files onto your device**.
- Under sync option, choose either **selected files** or **all files**.
- If you clicked on **Selected files,** then tick the boxes beside the files you wish to sync.
- Click on **Apply**

- Then click on **Sync** at the right bottom of the screen to sync your books between your mobile device and the Mac.

Sync Photos to your iPad or iPhone on Mac

Note: You will be unable to sync photos using your computer if you are using the iCloud Photo library sync on your iPad or iPhone.

- From your Dock, click on the Finder app.
- Click on the name of your device on the left side of your screen.
- Click on the **Photos** tab on the right side of your screen.
- Choose the files you wish to sync.
- Click on **Apply**
- Then click on **Sync** at the right bottom of the screen to sync your photos between your mobile device and the Mac.

Back-up your iPad or iPhone on macOS Catalina

Follow the steps below to manually backup your mobile device on your computer

- From your Dock, click on the Finder app.
- Click on the name of your device on the left side of your screen.

- Click on the **General** tab on the right side of your screen.
- Then click on **Back Up Now** besides the option for **Backup and Restore.**

Restore your iPad or iPhone on Mac

Follow the steps below to restore your mobile device on your computer manually

- From your Dock, click on the Finder app.
- Click on the name of your device on the left side of your screen.
- Click on the **General** tab on the right side of your screen.
- Then click on **Restore Back-Up** beside the option for Backup and Restore.

Chapter 4: Music App

Apple split iTunes into three different applications: Podcast, Music app, and Apple TV apps. If you use iTunes a lot, you might not experience difficulty in using the music app as the functions are alike.

Using Apple Music in the Music App

- Go to the Applications folder or navigate from your Dock to open the Music app.
- ➢ From the sidebar, click on **'For You'** to see the Apple suggestions and Mixes, playlists, and albums recently played as well as what your friends are playing.

- ➢ From the sidebar, click on **Browse** to go through currently trending artists, other available music in the Apple library as well as Apple's playlist selections.

➢ From the sidebar, click on **Radio** to find and play Beats 1 radio shows whether previously recorded or currently live.

- From the Radio section, click on **Featured** to view featured radio stations, Apple's highlighted Beats 1 streams, and radio contents recently played.

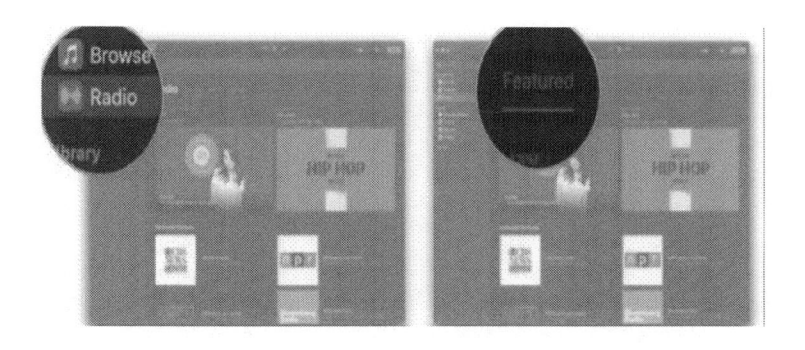

- To access and play Beats 1 contents, go to the Radio section and click on **Beats 1**
- For available radio stations in the Apple music as well as selected partners, go to the Radio section and click on **Stations.**

- If you find any song you want to add to your library, use the + button beside the album, song, or playlist.

Play Music in the Music App
- Go to the Applications folder or go from your Dock to open the Music app.
- Hover on a playlist or album to see the **Play** button. Tap the Play button.

- To play a particular song, click on the playlist or album.
- Then tap the **play** button.

Access Your Music Library in the Music App

- Go to the Applications folder or from your Dock to open the Music app.
- ➢ From the sidebar, click on **Recently Added** to view songs and albums (minus playlists) added to your library.
- From the same sidebar, click on **Artists** to look through the musical artists that own music in your library.
- Select **View** from the menu bar.
- Hover your mouse over the **Sort Albums By** option.
- Select either **Genre, Rating, Title, or Year.**
- Tap either **Descending** or **Ascending**, and you are done!

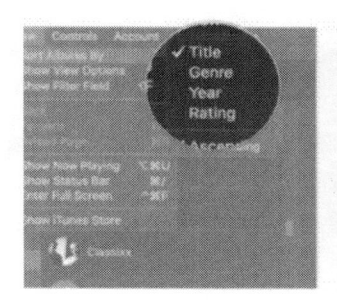

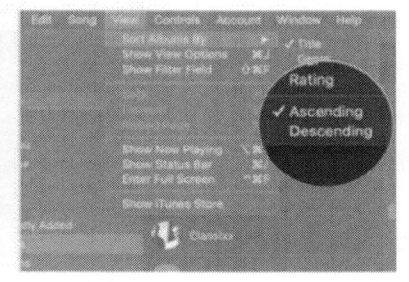

➢ To look through your music by the albums, go to the sidebar and click on **Albums.**

- Select **View** from the menu bar.

- Then click on **Show View Options**.
- From the drop-down list, you can choose to **sort by** the following**:** Title, Year, Artist, Genre, or Rating.

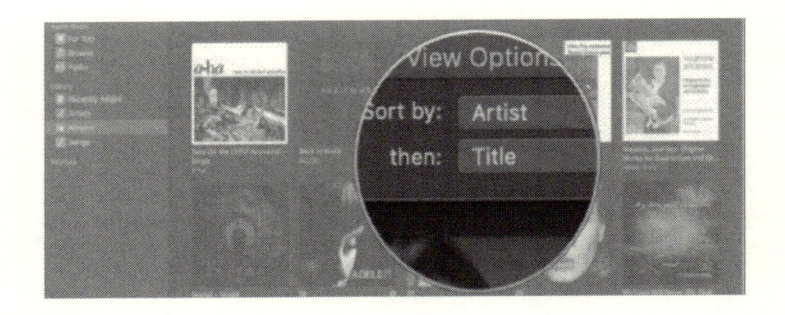

- Then go to **"Then"** and select from the options Title, Year, Artist, or Rating.

- ➢ To view all your songs, click on **Songs** from the sidebar.
- • You can then choose to sort your sorts by choosing from the available categories: **Name, Artist, Time, Genre, Album.**
- ➢ From the sidebar, click on a **Playlist** to open it. You will see the available playlists sorted by their origin in the sidebar. Playlists created from iTunes will come first, then the ones you created or subscribed to from the Apple Music will follow in alphabetical order.

Get Album and Song Info in the Music App

- • Open the Music app from the Application folder or your dock.
- • Control or right-click on an album or song.
- • Then click on **Get Info**

- When editing more than one song, select **Edit Items**

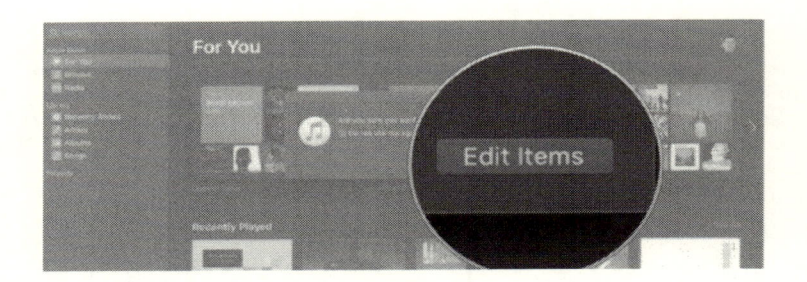

- You can choose to edit information saved under **Details, Lyrics, Artwork, Sorting, Options,** and **File** tabs
- Once done with the editing, click on **OK**

Import Music into the Music App

- Open the Music app from the Application folder or your dock.
- Click on **File**
- Then click on **Import**

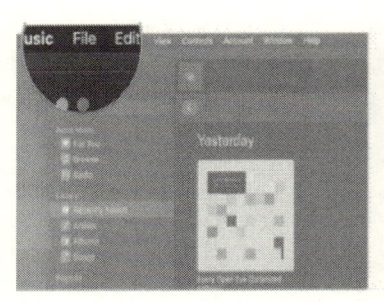

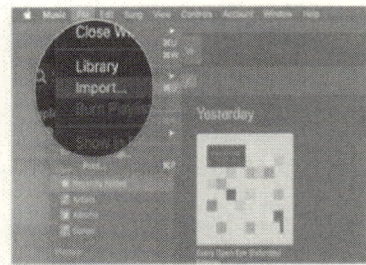

- Select the folder or file you wish to import.
- Then click on **Open**

General Settings in the Music App

- Open the Music app from the Application folder or your dock.
- Select **Music** from the menu bar

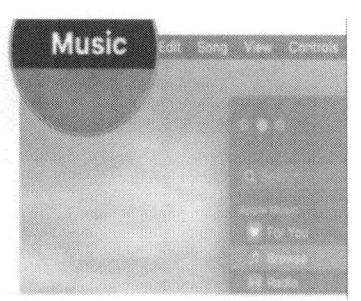

- Click on **Preferences.**
- Go to the **General** tab and tick the boxes to enable **Automatic Downloads,** turn on **iCloud Music Library**, and **Always check for available downloads**.
- Tick the boxes to hide or show Star Ratings, iTunes Store, Song list checkboxes.
- Click on the **drop-down** to choose the list size.

- Use the checkbox beside **Notification** to choose whether or not you want to receive notifications **when Songs Change.**

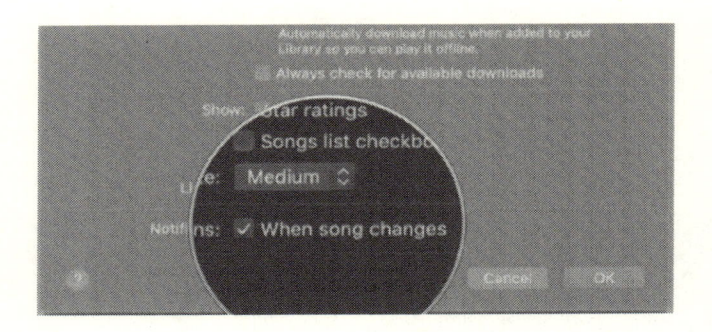

Playback Settings in the Music App

- Open the Music app from the Application folder or your dock.
- Select **Music** from the menu bar
- Click on **Preferences.**
- Then click on **Playback.**
- Tick the box beside **Crossfade Songs** to activate crossfading.
- Use the slider to go right or left to set how long you want the crossfade to last.
- Tick the box beside **Sound Enhancer.**
- Use the slider to go right or left and set the sound enhancement to high or low

- Tick the box beside **Sound Check** to activate Soundcheck.

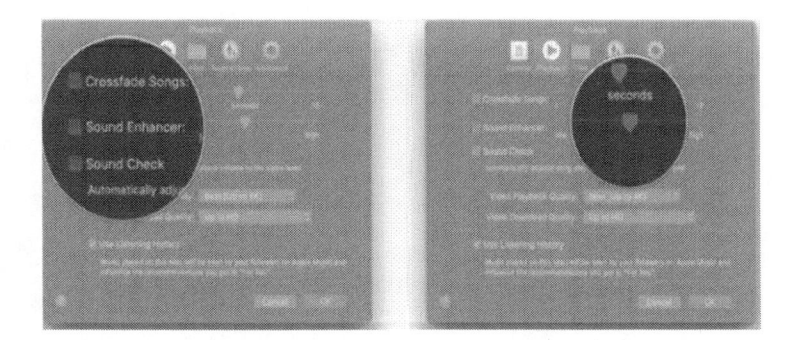

- Use the drop-down menu on the next screen to select the quality of your videos when playing or the allowed quality when downloading videos.
- Tick the box beside **Use Listening History** to show your played music to your friends and followers as well as receive recommendations following the types of music you listen to on your computer.

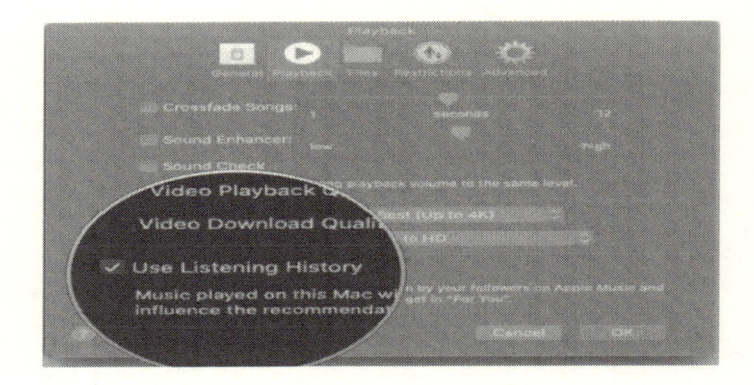

Setting up Parental Controls in the Music App

- Open the Music app from the Application folder or your dock.
- Select **Music** from the menu bar.
- Click on **Preferences.**
- Then click on **Restrictions**

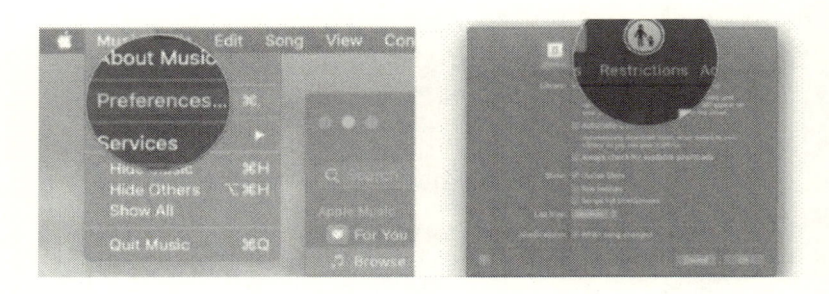

- (Un)tick the boxes **beside iTunes Store, Music Profiles, Apple Music, and Shared Libraries** to enable or disable.

- Click the next drop-down button for **'Ratings For'** to pick your preferred country rating.

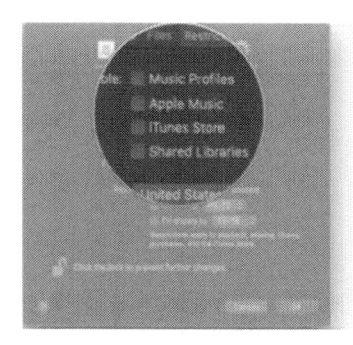

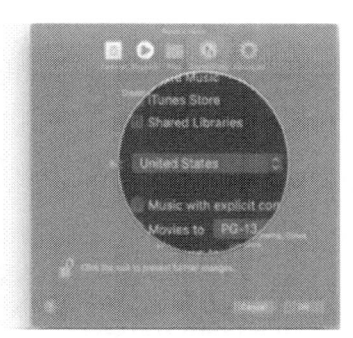

- Beside the boxes for **Restrict,** tick the box to restrict **"music with explicit content."**
- Then select your desired maximum content rating from the drop-down.

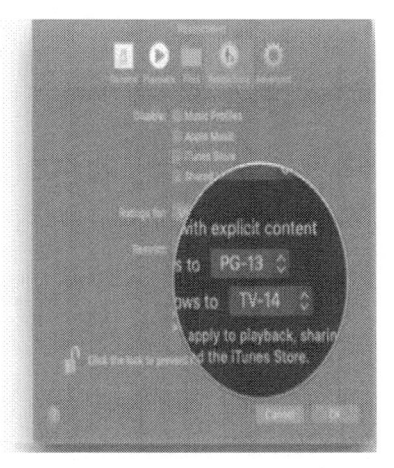

Music File Settings

To manage the music file settings, follow the steps below:

- Open the Music app from the Application folder or your dock.
- Select **Music** from the menu bar
- Click on **Preferences.**
- Then click on **Files**

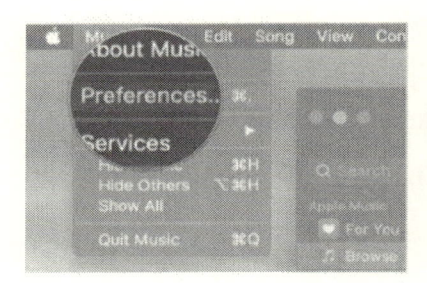

- Select **Change** if you will want to change the folder where the media is stored.
- Use the pop-up window to choose a different folder for storing media in the music app.
- Then click on **Open.**
- Return to **Preferences** and tick the box beside the "**Keep Music Media folder**

organized" to have your music organized in the preferred library folder.

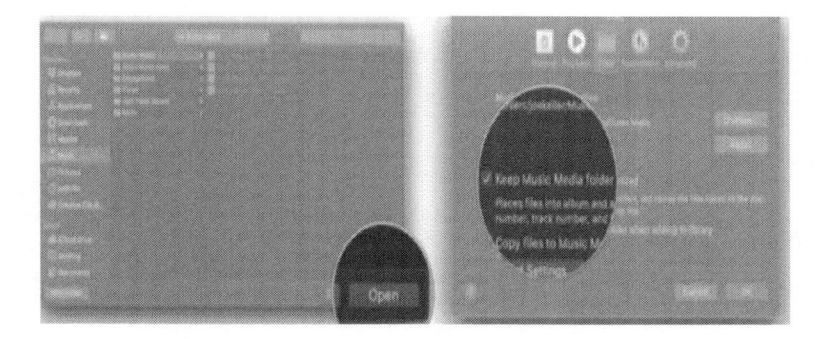

- Tick or untick the box beside **"Copy files to Music Media folder when adding to library"** to automatically add files that you drag into your library to the media folder.
- Then click on **Import Settings**.

- Click on the drop-down button to confirm the encoder format the imported files should come in: either **AAC, MP3, AIFF, Apple Lossless,** or **WAV**

- Then use the next drop-down to set up the quality of the encoding.

Reset Warnings in the Music App

- Open the Music app from the Application folder or your dock.
- Select **Music** from the menu bar
- Click on **Preferences.**
- Then click on **Advanced.**

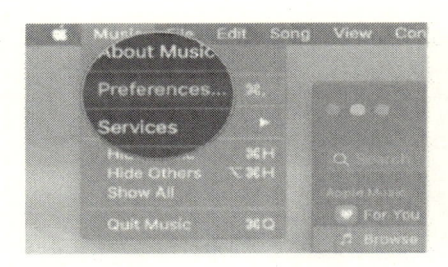

- Tick the boxes for **"Automatically update artwork"** and **"Add songs to Library when adding to playlists."**
- Then click on **Reset Warnings**.
- After which, you click on **Reset Cache**.

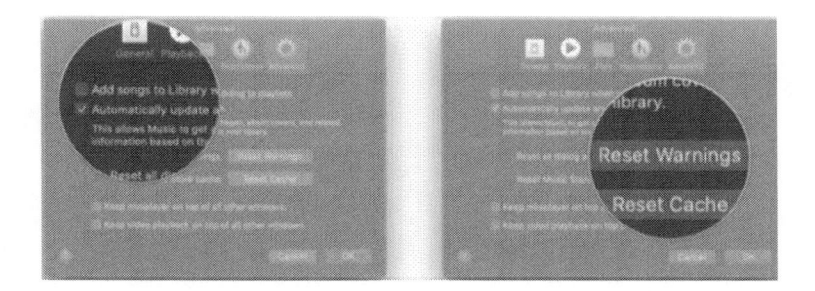

- Check the boxes for **"Keep video playback on top of all other windows"** and **"Keep mini-player on top of all other windows."**

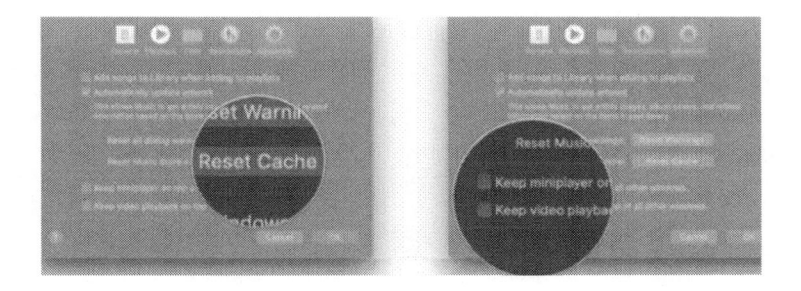

Chapter 5: Podcasts App on Mac

The Podcast app is another segment broken out of iTunes. The app allows you to search for, subscribe to and manage your podcast library. The app interface is similar to that of the iOS podcast app. The steps will guide you on everything regarding podcasts on your computer.

Play a Podcast in the Podcast App

It is quite easy to play a podcast, whether downloaded or not.

- You can open the podcasts app from the launchpad, Dock, or application folder.
- Then click on the podcast photo of your desired podcast.
- Regardless of the tab you are in at the time, whether searching for a new podcast or looking for your last podcast, whenever you click on a podcast, the app will automatically begin to play the podcast.

Search for Podcast from your Podcast Library

Follow the steps below to find an episode of a podcast available in your library.

- Open the podcasts app from the launchpad, Dock, or application folder.
- From the sidebar, click on the search bar.

- Then click on **Your Library**.
- Input your search keyword.
- Then click **Enter** on your keyboard.

Search for a Podcast from the App

You can use the search bar to find a new podcast.

- Open the podcasts app from the launchpad, Dock, or application folder.
- From the sidebar, click on the search bar.

- Input your search keywords.
- Then click **Enter** on your keyboard.
- The next screen will show all the available options for the episodes and shows related to the search keyword.

Subscribe to a Podcast

When you subscribe to a podcast, the podcast will automatically add to your library. This means that you will always see new episodes and be able to listen to them as they are released.

- Open the podcasts app from the launchpad, Dock or application folder.
- Search for the podcast you desire to subscribe to.

- Hover your mouse over the **Podcast photo** until you see the **Play and Option** button.
- Then click on **Options** (this is the 3 dots on your screen as shows in the screenshot below)
- Click on **Subscribe.**

Unsubscribe to a Podcast

You can choose to unsubscribe from a podcast whenever you want. It will not remove the podcast from your library but new episodes will not be automatically added to your library.

- Open the podcasts app from the launchpad, Dock or application folder.
- Search for the podcast you desire to unsubscribe in your library

- Hover your mouse over the **Podcast photo** until you see the **Play and Option** button.
- Then click on **Options** (this is the 3 dots on your screen as shows in the screenshot below)

- Click on **Unsubscribe.**

Play a Podcast Next in Queue from the App
- Open the podcasts app from the launchpad, Dock or application folder.

- Search for the podcast episode you desire to play next in your library
- Hover your mouse over the **Podcast photo** until you see the **Play and Option** button.
- Then click on **Options** (this is the 3 dots on your screen as shows in the screenshot below)
- Click on **Play Next.**

Delete a Podcast from Your Podcast Library

- Open the podcasts app from the launchpad, Dock or application folder.
- Search for the podcast you desire to delete in your library
- Hover your mouse over the **Podcast photo** until you see the **Play and Option** button.

- Then click on **Options** (this is the 3 dots on your screen as shows in the screenshot below)
- Click on **Delete from library.**

Share a Podcast in the App

Follow these steps to share podcast to your friend via email, messages, Notes, AirDrop or any other preferred method.

- Open the podcasts app from the launchpad, Dock or application folder.
- Look for the podcast you wish to share.
- Hover your mouse over the **Podcast photo** until you see the **Play and Option** button.
- Then click on **Options** (this is the 3 dots on your screen as shows in the screenshot below)
- Click on **"Share Show"** or **"Share Episode."**

72

- Select your preferred sharing method.
- Depending on the selected method, you may need to type in some more info. This is different for each method.

View Top Charts in the Podcasts App

From your podcast app, you can update yourself with what is trending and hot in the podcast world.

- Open the podcasts app from the launchpad, Dock or application folder.
- From the sidebar, click on **Top Charts**.

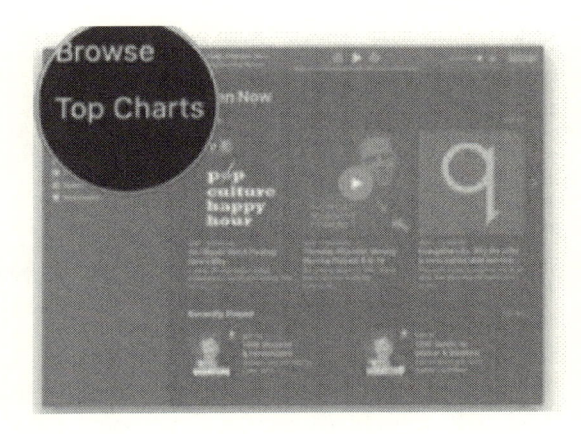

- The screen will display the top shows and episodes of podcasts that other Podcasts users are listening to.

Change the Play Order of Episodes
- Open the podcasts app from the launchpad, Dock, or application folder.
- Go to your library and look for any podcast that you will not want to receive its notifications.
- Hover your mouse over the **Podcast photo** until you see the **Play and Options** button.

- Then click on **Options** (this is the three dots on your screen as shown in the screenshot below)
- Click on **Settings**.
- Select your desired options for the episodes. You can choose from any of the four options below: **Play Most Recent First, Play in Sequential Order, Custom Settings** or **Only Keep the Most Recent Episodes.**

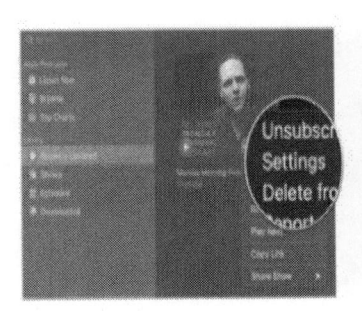

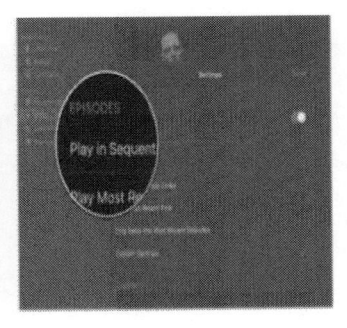

Chapter 6: Apple TV App for Mac

The Apple TV, which has been available on iOS, is now available on Mac too. You can watch your favorite channel titles or library right from your computer. Your progress on movies and shows will sync across your iPad, iPhone, Mac and the Apple TV so that you can always resume from the last watched content regardless of the device you are using. There is however one main difference between the TV app on your Mac and that of other Apple devices. The TV app on the Apple TV, iPad and iPhone integrates with several third-party apps like NBC and Hulu to give you multiple options in one single app. This feature, however, is not available with the TV app for your computer.

Play a Video from Your Library in the TV App

Thankfully, you no longer have to go to the separate TV shows and Movies app to watch the contents you purchased on the Apple TV.

- From the TV app, click on the **Library** located at the top side of your screen.

- You will see the following options in the sidebar:
➢ **TV Shows:** a collection of all your purchased TV shows
➢ **Movies:** a collection of all your purchased movies
➢ **Recently Added:** TV shows and movies that were added recently to your content library.
➢ **Genres:** choose from the available genres. Each genre has both TV shows and movies that belong to the chosen genre.
➢ **Downloaded:** TV shows and movies you downloaded to your computer to view when offline.

- Click on the show or movie you desire to watch.
- Hover your mouse on the chosen episode or movie until you see the play button. Click on the play button, and the show or TV will download and begin to play.

Watch a Movie or Show in the TV App

Follow the simple steps below to get started.
- Launch the TV app from the applications folder or your Dock.
- Click on a movie or TV show from the **Up Next** section to start watching it instantly.
- You can also navigate to **What to Watch** or any other section for movies and TV.

- Click on your preferred movie or show.
- Then click the **Play** button.

Add Movies and Shows to Up Next

When searching for what to watch on the TV app, your first stop should be **Up Next.** It gives you the latest episodes of your most loved shows or helps you resume the last movie you were watching.

- Launch the TV app from the applications folder or your Dock.
- Play a TV show or movie from the app to add the film to the **Up Next** section.
- Otherwise, you can click on a movie or content in any of the sections under **Up Next**
- Then click on **Add to Up Next**.

Buy TV Shows and Movies in the TV app

Apart from watching the contents that you have bought in the past, you can also buy TV shows and movies in your app.

- From the TV app, click on **TV Shows** or **Movies** at the top of your screen.
- Select the title you wish to rent or buy.
- Click on **Rent** or **Buy** once it is available.
- Alternatively, use the search bar and type the name of your desired title.
- Select the title from the search results.
- Click on **Rent** or **Buy** once it is available.

Subscribe to a Channel in the TV App

Similar to what you have on the Apple TV, iPad, or iPhone, You can also subscribe to channels like the Cinemax, EPIX, and Showtime.

- Go to the TV app.
- Under **Apple TV Channels,** click on the channel you wish to subscribe to.
- Then select **Try It Free.**
- Input your password.
- Then click on **Buy.**

- Click on **Confirm** to accept.
- After the free trial period, you will begin to get charged for the subscription. You will also receive content recommendations

from channels in the **Watch Now** part of the TV app.

Cancel a Channel Subscription on Your Mac

To cancel a free trial or unsubscribe from a channel, follow the steps below

- Go to **System Preferences** from the application folder or Dock
- Click on **Apple ID**.
- Select **Media & Purchases.**
- Beside **Subscriptions,** click on **Manage.**
- Besides **channel subscription,** click on **Edit** on your list of active subscriptions. When canceling during a free trial, you will find this at the end of the list.
- Click on **Cancel Subscription**.
- Then click on **Confirm** to accept.

Video Playback Settings in the TV App

- From the Apple TV app, click on TV in the menu bar.
- Click on **Preferences.**
- Then select **Playback.**

- Beside **Streaming Quality,** click on the drop-down to set the streaming media quality to either Good or Best Available.
- Beside **Download Quality,** click on the drop-down to set the streaming media quality to either **Up to SD, Up to HD, Up to SD,** or **Most Compatible Format.**
- Tick the boxes to set if the TV apps should download HDR content and multichannel audio.
- Tick the boxes if you want the TV app to be able to use your view history to set recommendations.

Downloads in the TV Apps
- From the TV app, click on **TV** in the menu bar.
- Select **Preferences**.
- If you want the app to always look for available downloads, go to the **General** section and then tick the box beside **Always check for available downloads.**

- You can choose to select both or either the **TV Shows** and **Movies** boxes to automatically download both or automatically download only TV episodes or movies.
- Tick the box beside "Checkboxes in Library" to automatically sync only items in your library that you have checked.
- Tap the drop-down button to select a new list size.

Manage Media Files in the TV App
- From the Apple TV app, click on TV in the menu bar.
- Click on **Preferences.**
- Then select **Files**.
- To change the folder where media contents are stored in the TV app, click on **Change** or click on **Reset** to return the folder to its default location.

- If changing the folder, choose a different folder for media storage from the pop-up window.
- Then click on **Open.**
- Return to **Preferences,** tick or untick the box beside **Keep Media folder organized** to have your media organized in the new library folder.
- Tick or untick the box beside **"Copy files to Media folder when adding to library"** to automatically add files that you drag into your library to the media folder.
- Tick the last box if you want the TV shows and movie files to be automatically deleted once you are done watching them.

Reset Warnings, Clear Cache and Play History

- Open the TV app from the Application folder or your dock.
- Select **TV** from the menu bar
- Click on **Preferences.**
- Then click on **Advanced.**

- Then click on **Reset Warnings**.
- After this, you click on **Reset Cache**.
- And click on **Clear Play History**.

Setting up Parental Controls in the TV App

- From the Apple TV app, click on TV in the menu bar.
- Click on **Preferences.**
- Then click on **Restrictions.**
- Tick or untick the boxes beside **Shared Libraries** and **Purchasing or Subscription** to enable or disable.

- Click the next drop-down button for **'Ratings For'** to pick your preferred country rating.
- Beside the boxes for **Restrict,** tick the box to restrict TV shows and movies to defined ratings.
- Then use the drop-down to choose the maturity limits of ratings for TV shows and movies.

Chapter 7: Notes App on Mac

The Notes app allows you to save information quickly from a shopping list to thoughts and ideas. You can also secure your notes with a password to be viewed by only you. You can also sync your notes across all your Apple devices. The guides below will show you how to maximize the Notes app on your computer.

Starting a New Note

- Open the Note app from the Application folder or your dock.
- Then click on the button for **New Note** (a pencil icon in a square)
- You can also click on **File** from the menu bar at your screen top and then click on **New Note.**
- Begin writing on your note.

Make a Checklist

- Open the Note app from the Application folder or from your dock.

- Then click on the button for **New Note** (a pencil icon in a square)
- You can also click on **File** from the menu bar at your screen top and then click on **New Note**.
- Click on the checklist button (a checkmark icon in a circle)
- Then type in your first item.
  - Tap **Enter** on your keyboard to start a new checklist item automatically.

Reorder Checklist Notes
- Launch the checklist you wish to re-order from the notes app.
- Then click and hold down on the box beside the checklist item you desire to move.
- Pull the checklist item to your preferred position. Do this until you have arranged the list to your satisfaction.

Make a Dashed, Bulleted or Numbered Headings and List
- Open the Note app from the Application folder or from your dock.

- Then click on the button for **New Note** (a pencil icon in a square)
- You can also click on **File** from the menu bar at your screen top and then click on **New Note**.
- In the menu bar, click on **Format.**
- Select **Heading** from the drop-down list to convert the next line in the note into a heading.
- Tick either **Numbered List, Dashed List** or **Bulleted List** for your preferred list type.
- To stop writing in a list, tap the **Return** button on your keyboard while on a blank list item.

Create Password for Locked Notes

- Open the Note app from the Application folder or from your dock.
- Click on **Notes** from the menu bar and then click on **Preferences.**
- Click on **Set Password.**
- Then type in your new password.

- Type in the password again in the field for **Verify**.
- You can choose to set up a password hint.
- Then click on **Set Password**.

View Note Attachments

- Open the Note app from the Application folder or from your dock.
- In the toolbar, you will find the Attachment button, looks like 4-square, click on it.

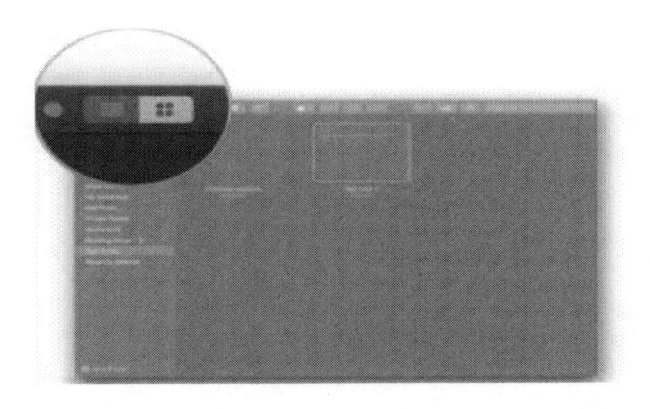

- Click on any of the different tabs like **Sketches, Photos & Videos**, and **Audio** to see your attachments.

Lock a Note

- From the Notes app, select the Note you want to lock.

- Navigate to the toolbar and click on the Lock icon, like a padlock image, to lock your Note.

Sign in to iCloud

- Open the **System Preferences** either from the Dock or go to the menu button at the left top side of your screen and then click on **System Preferences**.
- Select **iCloud**.

- Input your login credentials to sign in.
- Ensure to tick the box beside **Notes** under the iCloud menu after signing in.
- You can also sign into iCloud on your iPad and iPhones to sync your notes across all your devices.

Invite Others to Collaborate on a Note

macOS Catalina allows you to not only invite people to collaborate but to also work on a complete folder in the Notes app. Before you can collaborate on the note app, other invitees must be using iPhone, Mac or iPad.

- From the Notes app, open the Note you will like to add people to.
- In the toolbar, click on the button to Add people (a silhouette icon with a "+" beside it).

- Select either **Folder "[folder name]** or **Note "[note name]** to share that folder or note.
- Select the method to share the invite (a link, message, mail and so on)
- From the permission drop-down menu, chose what the invited persons can do with

the note, whether they can make changes or just read.
- Then click on **Share.**
- Input the phone number or email address of the persons you want to share the note with.
- Click on **Send.**

Send Note to Another App or Person
- Go to the notes app and select the notes for sharing.
- Tap the share button from the toolbar (this looks like a square with shooting out arrow)
- Select the app to use for sharing the note.

View Notes in a Gallery

With macOS Catalina, you have a gallery view that allows you to view your notes in a fashion that is more visually dynamic.
- First, open the notes app.
- Then launch the folder you will like to have the gallery view.

- At the left top side of the toolbar, click on the gallery button.
- You can return the folder to the list view by clicking on the List button.

Sync Notes to iCloud in macOS Catalina

- Go to System Preferences.
- Then click on **Apple Account**.

- Log in to your **iCloud account** if not logged in already.
- Then click on iCloud.
- Tick the box besides Notes if unchecked.

Chapter 8: Reminders App on Mac

In this part of the book, you will learn important aspects of the Reminders app on your computer. You can use the reminders app to create your shopping lists, track the most important tasks, and several other functions. The iCloud and other services can help to sync your to-do list across your iPad, iPhone and Mac devices.

Create a Reminder

- Go to your Dock and launch Reminders.
- Then click the plus "+" button.

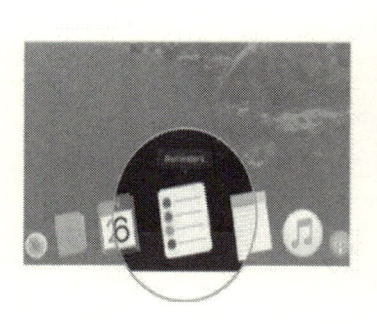

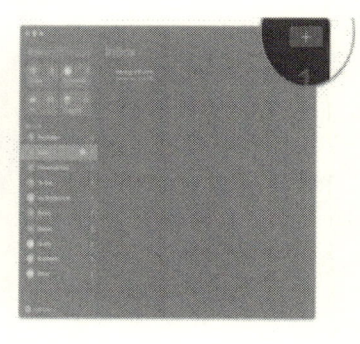

- Type your reminder and save

Add Reminders Account Provider

- Go to your Dock and launch Reminders

- Click on **Reminders** from the menu bar.

- Then click on **Add Account.**
- Select the Reminders account type you want, for example, iCloud.
- Then click on **Continue.**
- Input your login credentials then sign in.

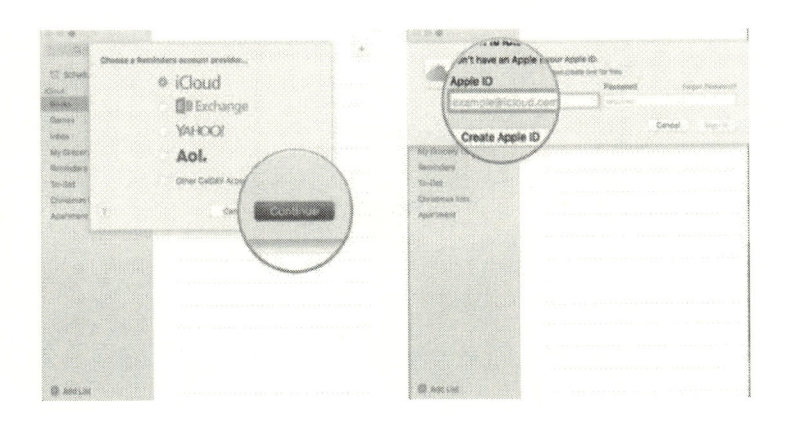

- Check that the box beside Reminders is ticked; if not, tick the box and choose the app you want your account to be used with.
- Then click on **Add Account.**

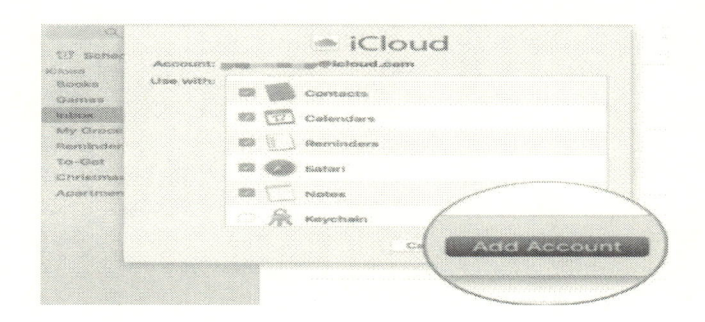

Setting up Location Notification for a Reminder

- Go to your Dock and launch Reminders.
- Select the text for the reminder you want to add the location.
- Then click on **Add Location.**
- You can either choose from the suggestions if it suits your needs or just your location manually.
- Then click on the suggestion that comes up on the list.

Schedule Due Date for a Reminder

- Go to your Dock and launch Reminders.

- Select the text for the reminder you want to add the date.
- Then click on **Add Date.**
- You can either choose from the suggestions or type your date.
- Then click on **Add Time.**
- Choose from the suggestions or type your preferred time.

Create a New List

- Go to your Dock and launch Reminders.
- Then click on **Add List.**
- Type your preferred name for the list.

Rename a List

- Go to your Dock and launch Reminders.
- Right-click with your mouse on the list you desire to rename.
- Then click on **Rename** and input the new name.

Delete a List

- Go to your Dock and launch Reminders.
- Right-click with your mouse on the list you desire to delete.

- Then click on **Delete**.

Share a List with Another iCloud User

- Go to your Dock and launch Reminders.
- Click with your mouse on the **Share** button beside the list you want to share. The share button will come up when you hover your cursor on the name of the existing list.
- Select the method you will like to share the list with, either Airdrop, Copy Link, Messages, or Mail.

- For Messages or Mails, click on **Share**.
- Input the name, phone number, or email address of the receiver.
- Then click on **Send**.

- If using **AirDrop** or **Copy Link,** Input the name, phone number, or email address of the receiver.

- Then click on **Share.**

Move a Reminder to another List

- Go to your Dock and launch Reminders.
- Click with your mouse on the list that has the reminder you want to move.
- Click and hold down on the reminder you want to move.
- Pull the reminder over the new list you want it at.

Using Text Snippets in Reminder

Before the launch of this current software, the Reminders app was nothing exciting. It was just the regular reminders app without any extra features. Now, the Reminders app has been completely redesigned to add some handy new features that were not there before. One of such features is being able to understand text snippets. Rather than typing your reminder, then manually set the location, time and other features, you can now type these details in natural language and they will be added automatically to the reminder. For instance, you can type, "Date with Michelle tomorrow at McDonald's for 5 pm," the reminders app will now create a reminder and also give you suggestions to set the time and date to tomorrow for 5 pm. This is pretty cool and simple.

Group Reminder Lists

- From the Reminders app, click and pull one list on another list.
- Then input a name for the new group.

Add a Message Notification for Reminders

This is similar to iOS 13. You can choose to receive notifications on a task the next time you message a specified contact.

- Hover your cursor on the reminder you wish to add to the message notification, then click on the "i" button that appears.

- Check the box beside **When Messaging a Person**.
- Type the contact's name or scroll through the list.
- Click on the desired contact.

Add Attachments to Reminder

- Hover your cursor on the reminder you wish to add to the message notification, then click on the "i" button that appears.

- Click on **Add Image**.

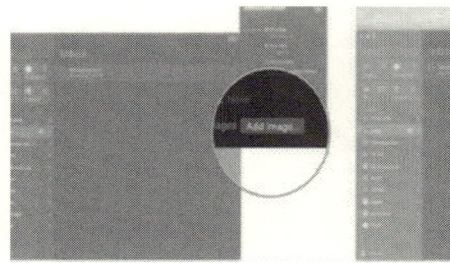

- Select **Photos** to go through your Photo library and add photos.
- Click either **Add Sketch**, **Scan Documents**, or **Take Photo** under the iOS devices to create images directly on the iOS device and import these images from the iOS device.

Add Secondary Reminder to an Existing one

Follow the steps below to create a sub-reminder under an existing one.

- Go to your Dock and launch Reminders.
- In the same list as the existing reminder, create another reminder.
- Click and hold down on the new reminder.
- Pull the new reminder to the existing reminder.
- Use the chevrons to hide or show the sub reminder

Chapter 9: Voice Controls on Mac

macOS Catalina allows you to control your computer with your voice through the use of speech commands. This new feature is beneficial to persons that have limited mobility, dexterity and other conditions. It is also another great way you can interact with your computer.

Turn on Voice Control

You have first to set up this feature to be able to enjoy the benefits. Follow the steps below:

- From the system Dock, click on **System Preferences**
- Tap on **Accessibility**.
- Under the section for Motor, click on **Voice Control** on the left side.
  - Then tick the box beside **Enable Voice Control** to activate this feature.

Change the Voice Control Language on Mac

This feature uses your computer's language as its default language when setting up. Follow the steps below to change this:

- From your system Dock, click on **System Preferences**
- Click on **Accessibility**.
- Under the section for Motor, click on **Voice Control** on the left side.
- Use the drop-down option besides Language.
- Click on **Customize.**
- Select the languages you wish to add.
- Then click on **OK.**

Sleep/ Wake Voice Control on Mac

- On the voice control icon on your screen, click on **Sleep** to put the tool to sleep. This means that voice control will not be active at this time.
- Click on **Wake** to bring out the feature from sleep.

Select New Language in Voice Control

- Go to the voice control icon and click on the current language on the right side of your screen.

- Select the new language.

Choose a Different Microphone for Voice Control

Voice Control uses the built-in microphone on your computer by default. You can select another microphone with the steps below:

- From the system Dock, click on **System Preferences**
- Tap on **Accessibility**.
- Under the section for Motor, click on **Voice Control** on the left.
- Navigate to **Microphone** and click on the pull-down menu.
- Select your desired microphone from the list.

Disable/ Enable Commands in Voice Control

Here, you will learn how to disable or enable any command available in voice control, whether you or Apple created them.

- From the system Dock, click on **System Preferences**
- Tap on **Accessibility**.
- Under the section for Motor, click on **Voice Control** on the left side.

- Select the **Command** button at the end of the page.
- (Un)tick the boxes for the commands you want to activate or disable.
- Then click on **Done.**

Create Custom Commands in Voice Control

Follow the steps below to add personal commands to the voice control feature:

- From the system Dock, click on **System Preferences**
- Tap **Accessibility.**
- Under the section for Motor, click on **Voice Control** on the left side.
- Select the **Command** button at the end of the page.
- Click on the plus (+) button.
- Go to the box for **'When I say'** and input your new commands. By default, this command will apply to all apps.

- If you want to use the new command on a specific app, click the pull-down menu beside **While Using**.
- Select the apps to use with the specified custom command.
- Go to the option for **Performed** and select your preferred option from the list.
- Then click on **Done.**

Delete Custom Commands in Voice Control

Follow the steps below to permanently delete a custom command in voice controls:

- From the system Dock, click on **System Preferences**
- Tap on **Accessibility**.
- Under the section for Motor, click on **Voice Control** on the left side.
- Select the **Command** button at the end of the page.
- Go to **Custom** and select the Command you wish to delete.
- Then click on the minus **"-"** button.

- And select **Delete** to confirm the action.

Receive an Alert for Recognized Commands in Voice Control

Your computer can alert you with a sound any time it recognizes a command. Follow the steps below to set up this feature:

- From the system Dock, click on **System Preferences**
- Tap on **Accessibility**.
- Under the section for Motor, click on **Voice Control** on the left side.
- Navigate to the bottom of the screen and tick the box beside **Play sound when command is recognized.**

Chapter 10: Using Sidecar on Mac

Another exciting feature introduced to iPadOS 13 and macOS Catalina is Sidecar. With Sidecar, you can extend the display of your computer to your iPad to enable you to use your Apple Pencil on your computer and perform your daily tasks like sketching and drawing or marking up screenshots. Sidecar allows you to use the default and 3rd party apps on your iPad like Affinity Photo, Adobe Illustrator, ZBrush, etc.

Requirements to Use Sidecar
- Your iPad and Mac must support Sidecar.
- You have to connect your iPad and Mac to the same iCloud account.
- Ensure that your iPad is on the most recent version of iPadOS.
- Turn on Wi-Fi, Bluetooth, and Handoff.
- Both devices should be placed within 30 feet (10 meters) of each other.
- The Computer should not be sharing its internet connection.
- The iPad should not be sharing its internet connection.

Setting up Sidecar on Mac

Before you can enjoy the features of Sidecar, you have to first activate it on Mac with the steps below:

- In the Dock of your Mac, click on **System Preferences**.
- Click on **Sidecar**.
- Navigate to the option for "Connect to" and tap the drop-down arrow for **Select Device**.
- Click on the name of your iPad from the menu.
- If your iPad doesn't show in the drop-down menu, you can try to plug your iPad into your computer and run the steps again.

Setting up Sidecar on your iPad

Currently, the only steps needed to set up Sidecar on iPad is to ensure that both the iPad and the Mac are connected through Bluetooth or directly and they are both on the same iCloud account. Apart from these, you do not need to perform any more steps to setup Sidecar on your iPad.

Customize Sidecar on your Computer

You can use Sidecar in different ways, you can choose to use the Sidebar on the right or left as well as deciding to show your computer Touch Bar on the bottom or the top of your computer, when applicable.

The steps below will show you how to customize these options:

- Go to **System Preferences** from the Dock of your Mac.
- Click on **Sidecar**
- (Un)tick the checkbox beside **Show Sidebar** to turn it off or on.
- If you turned on the option for **Show Sidebar,** use the toggle beside it to choose either **Right** or **Left.**
- (Un)tick the checkbox beside **Show Touch Bar** to turn it off or on, where applicable.
- If you turned on the option for **Show Touch Bar,** use the toggle beside it to choose either **Bottom** or **Top.**

Customizing Apple Pencil Options

You have two settings to customize for Apple Pencil on your computer:

- Go to **System Preferences** from the Dock of your Mac.
- Click on **Sidecar**
- (Un)tick the checkbox beside **Enable double tap on Apple Pencil** to turn it off or on.
- (Un)tick the checkbox beside **Show pointer when using Apple Pencil** to turn it off or on.

The iPad as a Graphics Tablet

You can work on your computer and make use of the iPad and Apple Pencil for your graphics needs.

- Connect your iPad and your Mac laptop to the same iCloud account.
- Launch a Mac app that integrates with Sidecar.
- With this, you can make use of your iPad and Apple pencil while using the design, drawing, or illustration apps on your Mac.

Chapter 11: Mail App

The Mail app on your computer allows you to use any email provider of your choice without the need to go to the individual provider's website. You can sync your Outlook account, school accounts, Gmail account, work account, etc. on the Apple Mail app, all you need to do is to set them up. In this chapter, I will show you how to do that.

Setting up an Email account
The first thing you need to do to use the Mail app is to set up your email accounts to begin receiving emails in the Mail app.

- Open the mail app from Finder or the Dock on your Mac.
- Click on the email provider for your type of email account. If the email account you are using is outside the options provided (like a work or school email address not owned by the big providers), select **Other Mail Account.**
- Tap **Continue.**
- Input your email address and password.

- On the next screen, tick the box beside each of the apps you want to use with the mail app. (Gmail, Yahoo, Outlook, AOL, etc.)
- Tap **Done.**
- To add more than one email account, repeat the process above to see all the email accounts in the Mail app.

Setting Frequency for Searching for New Messages

The Mail app goes to all the different providers to fetch your emails at intervals. Depending on your settings, this check can be done within seconds, minutes, hours or manually. Follow the steps below to customize how often the app should conduct this check:

- Open the mail app from Finder or the Dock on your Mac.
- Navigate to the menu bar located at the left top side of your screen and click on **Mail.**
- Select **Preferences.**
- It should take you to the **General tab,** if it doesn't, click on the General tab.
- Next to the option for **Check for new messages,** click the dropdown menu.

- Select your desired frequency.

Mail Notification Sounds
This step will guide you on setting a sound alert for incoming emails.

- Open the mail app from Finder or the Dock on your Mac.
- Navigate to the menu bar located at the left top side of your screen and click on **Mail.**
- Select **Preferences.**
- It should take you to the **General tab,** if it doesn't, click on the General tab.
- Next to the option for **New messages sound,** click the dropdown menu.
- Select your desired sound for incoming mail notification. When you click on a sound, you will hear a preview of the sound.

Add a Signature to your Emails
Your email signature shows under the body of your email every time you send an email. If you set up a signature to your email, you will never need to manually type in your name for each email you send.

- Open the mail app from Finder or the Dock on your Mac.
- Navigate to the menu bar located at the left top side of your screen and click on **Mail.**
- Select **Preferences.**
- Navigate to the **Signature** tab.
- Select the account you want to add the signature.
- At the lower center of the page, you will see the **+ button,** click on it.
- Navigate to the window on the far right to type in your signature.
- Then change the name of your signature by clicking the center window.
- Go to **Choose signature** and click on the dropdown menu.
- Select your preference from the 4 options on the list: At Random, None, In sequential order or the name of the new signature you created.

Sending a new Email
- Launch the mail app.
- Tap the **Compose** button.

- Input the receiver's email address. You can enter more than one email address.
- Type in the subject of your email.
- In the body of the new email, type in your message.
- Once done, click on the send button. This send button looks like a paper airplane located at the left top side of the message window.

Replying an Email
To reply a received email, follow the steps below:
- Launch the mail app.
- Open the email you want to send a reply.
- Then tap the reply button, this looks like a single curved arrow.
- If the email has more than one receipients, you can reply all the receipients by clicking on **Reply All,** a two-curved arrow icon.
- To forward the message to other people, click the **Forward button,** a right-pointing arrow icon beside the reply button.
- Write the content of your email and then click the send button.

Download and View Email Attachments

The steps below will guide you on how to download or view email attachments

- Open the mail app.
- Open the received email that has the attachment.
- Double-click on the document in the email to view it. You will see the photos appear in the body of your email.
- Move your mouse over the white area following From and To.
- Beside the number, a little menu will pop up, click on the downward arrow.
- Tap the name of the attached file.
- Tap **Save** after you must have selected the save location and setting the file to suit your preference.

Searching for Specific Email Messages

- Open the mail app.
- Navigate to the right top side of your window and click on the search bar.
- Type your search term, be it name, subject, email address or even specific words from an email.

- You may also select a search option that appears in the drop-down.
- You may also click on a folder to search, this is optional. You have the option to search all folders or specific folders.
- Select the email you want to view.

Filter Email by Unread
If you have lots of received email, it may be hard to know the ones that you have read and the unread ones. Good news is, you can filter your received emails by Unread.

- Open the mail app.
- Navigate to the menu bar located at the left top side of your screen and click on **View.**
- Select **Sort By.**
- Then click on **Unread.**

Another way you can do this is to click the filter button beside **Sort By,** located at the top of the inbox section. This will automatically show you your unread emails.

Mark an Email as Unread

If there is an email that you have read but will like to go back to it later, you can mark it as unread so as not to get lost in the inbox.

- Open the mail app.
- Go to the email you want to mark as Unread and right-click on the email.
- From the drop-down, select **Mark as Unread.**

Another way to do this is, if you use a magic mouse, swipe to the right of the email and select **Unread**, similar to the iPad or iPhone.

Deleting an Email

Follow the steps below to delete emails you no longer need.

- Open the mail app.
- Tap the email you want to delete. For multiple messages, click on one, then hold the shift key and click on another message. This action will

automatically select all the messages between each of the selected emails.
- Navigate to the top of the page and click on the **Delete** button to move the mails to the trash can.

Apple Mail Flag Feature
The flag feature in the mail app is used to mark important email messages that you intend to go back to in the future. The steps below will guide you on how to use this feature

- Select an email in the mail app
- Right click on the email, then click on **Flag,** from the displayed menu
- Then tap the **Flag** icon located at the top of the inbox.
- Open the message menu, choose **Flag**
- Then press **Command-L-Shift** keys on your keyboard

Unsubscribe from a Mailing List in Mail
As long as we have active email accounts, we will always be tempted to sign up for several email lists. After some time, we begin to receive emails that are no longer of interest to us but unfortunately, it is not every email

sender that makes it easy for receivers to remove themselves from these mailing lists. Thankfully, with macOS Catalina, you can unsubscribe from these mailing lists directly in the mail app.

Each time you receive an email from a mailing list, the Mail app will include a bar at the top of the received email that reads, **"This message is from a mailing list,"** and will also include the "Unsubscribe" link. If you are no longer interested in that mailing list, click on the "Unsubscribe" link to unsubscribe. This works as long as the Mail app can identify every email coming from a mailing list.

Block a Sender in Mail

If you will rather not receive emails from a particular sender and want to move all their sent emails to Trash, go to the email received from the sender and click on their name in the email header. The option to block will pop up. Click on it to block the sender.

Sign Documents on Your Computer with your iPad or iPhone in Quick Look

- Click on the Finder icon to launch the Finder window on your computer.
- Locate the file you wish to sign and click once on it.
- Tap space bar on your computer's keyboard. You will see your document appear in **Quick Look.**
- Select the **Markup** button (a pencil-like icon).
- Then click on the **Signature** button.
- Select **iPhone or iPad**.
- Then click on **Select Device**.
- From the list of devices, choose your iPad or iPhone.
- Sign your signature on your iPad or iPhone.
- Then click on **Done** from your iPad or iPhone device.
- The signature will appear on your computer's signature menu. Select the signature.

- Pull the signature and drop it in its right place on document.
- Then click on **Done.**

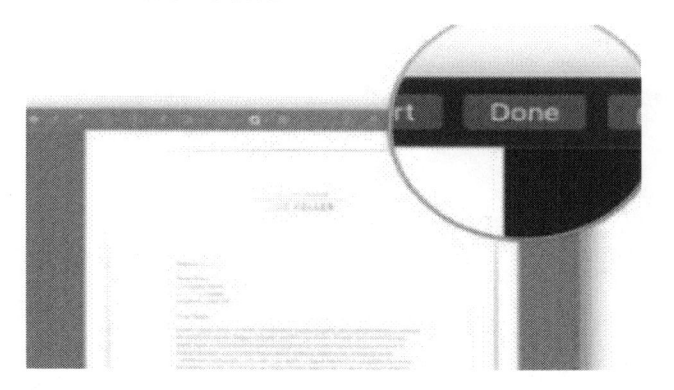

Sign Documents on Your Computer with your iPad or iPhone in Preview

- Go to **Preview** on your computer.
- Launch the document that needs the signature.
- Click on **View.**
- Then click on **Show Markup Toolbar** from the drop-down list.

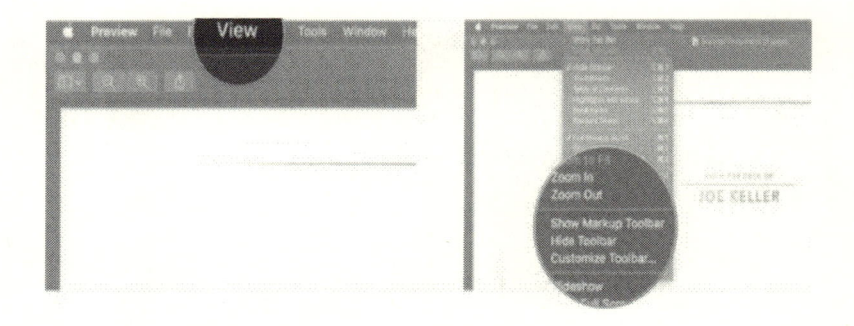

- Click on the signature button.
- Select **iPhone or iPad**.
- Then click on **Select Device**.
- From the list of devices, choose your iPad or iPhone.
- Sign your signature on your iPad or iPhone device.
- Then click on **Done** from your iPad or iPhone.
- The signature will appear on your computer's signature menu. Select the signature.
- Pull the signature and drop it in its right place on document.
- Then click on **Save** to save the document.

Chapter 12: Safari on Mac

Safari is the default web browser for the Apple devices for surfing the net. The guide below will show you how to use it on your computer. Safari is used to grant you access to any website you wish to view so long as you have the web address.

Steps to Use Picture-in-Picture Feature in Safari

This feature is Apple-Speak that allows you to run a video in its window while running another app. It can be beneficial for multitasking. For instance, you can be watching an important event while also working on the Notes app. This feature has also been added to Safari; you can watch a video in Safari while operating another app. The step to do this is straightforward.

- Go to the page that has the video
- Click and hold the **Volume** icon located in the navigation bar.
- This will display a menu.
- Click on **Enter Picture in Picture** to pull the video into its separate window.

- Set to your preferred size and move to the edge of your screen.

Visit a Website
- Open the Safari browser from the Finder or the Dock.
- Tap the address bar at the top of the page.
- Input your desired address, e.g. www.google.com
- Tap the **Return** key on your keyboard.

Bookmark a Website

For faster access to your most loved sites, add the website address to bookmark so that you can click on it to return to the website at any time.
- Open the Safari browser from the Finder or the Dock.
- Navigate to the web page you want to add to the bookmark.
- Press both **Command-D** keys on your keyboard.

- Title your bookmark or leave it with the default title. Input a description if you desire.
- Then tap the **Return** or **Add** key on your keyboard.
- Go to the menu bar located at the left top of your screen.
- Then click on **Show Favorites Bar**.
- You will see the bookmarked pages under the address bar. Click on it to access it. Also, whenever you click on the address bar, you will find your favorite pages listed under suggested sites.

Searching on the Address Bar

Apart from inputting the website address, you can also input keywords on the address bar to search for your inquiry on Google.

- Open the Safari browser from the Finder or the Dock.
- Tap the address bar at the top of the page.
- Type in your desired query like "release date for the macOS Catalina."

- Tap the **Return** key on your keyboard.
- Safari will then take you to Google, where you will see multiple results for your query.

Remove Bookmarks

Follow the steps below to remove a bookmarked page from your favorites or bookmarks

- Open the Safari browser from the Finder or the Dock.
- At the top left of your screen, click on **Bookmarks** from the menu bar.
- Then click on **Edit Bookmarks**.
- Tap the arrow beside **Favorites** as that is where the bookmarks are by default.
- Control-click or right-click on the bookmark you want to delete.
- Then select **Delete.**

View All Bookmarks

Follow the steps below to view all your bookmarks in one single view

- Open the Safari browser from the Finder or the Dock.

- Besides the address bar, click on the button for **Show sidebar.**
- Tap the bookmarks tab if it is not already showing (this is an open book icon)

Add a Web Page to your Reading List

When you add pages to your reading lists, you can save the site for reading later. You can also access the reading list even if there is no active internet connection.

- Open the Safari browser from the Finder or the Dock.
- Navigate to the website you wish to add to your reading list.
- Then tap **shift-command-D** keys on your keyboard.
- You will notice a small icon at the sidebar button or the sidebar itself.

Enable Private Browsing

When using private browsing, you can surf the internet without the computer saving your search history, sites visited, or having the AutoFill information. This is ideal when you do not want anyone to access your browsing data.

- Open the Safari browser from the Finder or the Dock.
- Go to the left top of your screen and click on **File** in the menu bar.
- Select **New Private Window** from the drop-down menu.
- Another way is to tap the **shift-command-N** keys on your keyboard.

View Your Reading List

- Open the Safari browser from the Finder or the Dock.
- Besides the address bar, tap the **reading list tab,** an icon similar to a pair of glasses.
- Select the item you wish to read to begin reading.

Remove items from your Reading Lists

Follow the steps below to remove items you no longer need from your reading list.

- Open the Safari browser from the Finder or the Dock.

- Besides the address bar, tap the **Show sidebar**.
- Click the tab for the **reading list;** the icon is similar to a pair of glasses.
- Control-click or right-click on the item you want to delete.
- Then select '**Remove Item**.'

Add Extensions to Safari

These are plug-ins that give additional functions to the browser. You can use it to integrate the browser with apps, block ads, and other functions. There are several free extensions that you can use to be current with news, increase productivity, provide entertainment and security, and lots more. Please note that some of the services or apps that provide these extensions may not be free even if the extension itself is free.

- Open the Safari browser from the Finder or the Dock.
- Go to the left top of your screen and click on **Safari** in the menu bar.
- Then click on **Safari Extensions**.

- You will be taken to the App Store's Safari extension page.
- Here you can now download and install extensions in the same manner as if you were downloading an app.
- Once the installation is complete, launch the app to add it to the toolbar in Safari.

Pin Tabs on Safari

This is similar to adding sites to your bookmarks. This feature will pin the tabs to your browser home page so that you can click on it for fast access.

- Open the Safari browser from the Finder or the Dock.
- Go to the left top of your screen and click on **View** in the menu bar.
- Then select **Show Tab Bar** from the drop-down.
- Navigate to the website you want to pin down.
- Click and hold down on the website tab and move it to the left side.

- You will see the tab showing the first letter of the site title or as a little site logo on the left side of the tab bar.
- Move the tab to the right to remove it from the pinned tabs list.

Setting Browser Homepage

When you launch your Homepage, it will take you directly to apple.com. But you can choose a different website to show when you start your browser.

- Open the Safari browser from the Finder or the Dock.
- Go to the left top of your screen and click on **Safari** in the menu bar.
- Go to the tab for **General.**
- Besides the option for **Homepage,** input a website address.
- Or, you can select **"Set to Current Page"** to use the current page on your browser as your homepage.
- Besides the option for **New windows open with,** tap the dropdown menu.

- If you will prefer that a new window opens on your homepage, click on **Homepage.**
- Besides the option for **New tabs open with**, tap the dropdown menu.
- If you will prefer that new tabs open on your homepage, click on **Homepage.**

Reader View

When using reader view, you can pull up web pages in a way that will make it easy to see images and read words without all the programmed movements or animations on the page. Most web pages support this view.

- Go to a website you want to view.
- Click on the button for **Reader View;** this is the lines you see on the left side of the address bar.

Share Websites from Safari

Follow the steps below to share a website with family or friends:

- Open the Safari browser from the Finder or the Dock.

- Navigate to the website you want to share.
- You will find the **Share** button at the right top of your screen, click on it.
- Select a method to share the site, either Notes, Emails, AirDrop, Messages, Reminders, or any other supported Non-Apple sites.

Change Background Color in Reader View
- Go to a website you want to view.
- Click on the button for **Reader View;** this is the lines you see on the left side of the address bar.
- Then tap the **Reader Options** button (this is the AA icon at the right of the address bar)
- Select your preferred background color.

Modify Font Size in Reader View
- Go to a website you want to view.
- Click on the button for **Reader View;** this is the lines you see on the left side of the address bar.

- Then tap the **Reader Options** button (this is the AA icon at the right of the address bar).
- Click the smaller "A" icon to reduce text size and the bigger A to increase the text size.

Modify Font in Reader View
- Go to a website you want to view.
- Click on the button for **Reader View;** this is the lines you see on the left side of the address bar.
- Then tap the **Reader Options** button (this is the AA icon at the right of the address bar)
- Select your preferred font.

Customize Favorites in Safari

Follow the steps below to add a website to your list of favorites

- Go to the desired website in Safari.
- Move your pointer on the Smart Search Field.
- Then click on **Favorites.**

If you want to remove a website from your list of favorites, follow the steps below:

- Go to the Safari toolbar and click on **Bookmarks.**
- Then click on **Show Favorites.**
- Use your mouse to right-click on the website you want to take out from the list.
- Then click on **Delete.**

Organize Your Safari Favorites

- Go to the Safari toolbar and click on **Bookmarks.**
- Then click on **Show Favorites.**
- Move the Favorite to your desired location on the list.

Organize Frequently Visited in Safari

With macOS Catalina, Safari adds websites automatically to your Frequently visited list. Follow the steps below to remove any site from this list

- Go to the Safari toolbar and click on **Bookmarks.**
- Click on **Show Favorites.**
- Then click on **Show Frequently Visited in Favorites** on the same drop-down.

Follow the steps below to delete a frequently visited site

- Launch your browser, then go to the Favorites page.
- You will see frequently visited sites. Right-click on the site you wish to delete.
  - Then click on **Delete.**

Access Siri Suggestions

- Go to the Safari toolbar and click on **Bookmarks**.
- Then click on **Show Favorites**.
- Navigate to Siri Suggestions on the next screen and click on any desired web page.

Chapter 13: Conclusion

With all the teachings in this book, I am confident that you will be able to fully enjoy all the fantastic features of the macOS Catalina on your Mac.

I have ensured that everything you need to know regarding the macOS Catalina is covered in this book to help you maximize your experience on your Mac

If you are pleased with the content of this book, don't forget to recommend this book to a friend.

Thank you.

Other Books by The Same Author

- The iPhone XS AND XS MAX USER GUIDE
  https://amzn.to/2kgrHJ2
- The iPhone XR User Guide
  https://amzn.to/2miQay8
- THE IPHONE X USER GUIDE
  https://amzn.to/2lQE6Uw
- Samsung Galaxy Note 10 User Guide
  https://amzn.to/2MbH3d9
- iPhone 11 User Guide
  https://amzn.to/32bObMa
- iPhone 11 Pro User Guide
  https://amzn.to/2nGAvtz
- iPhone 11 Pro Max User Guide
  https://amzn.to/2MBLixt
- Mastering the iOS 13
  https://amzn.to/2MHlr7A

Made in the USA
Middletown, DE
09 November 2021